T0246240

THE
LITTLE
HISTORY
OF
WORCESTERSHIRE

THE
LITTLE
HISTORY
OF
WORCESTERSHIRE

VANESSA
MORGAN

The
History
Press

First published 2023

The History Press
97 St George's Place, Cheltenham,
Gloucestershire, GL50 3QB
www.thehistorypress.co.uk

British Library Cataloguing in Publication Data.
A catalogue record for this book is available from the British Library.

ISBN 978 1 80399 120 7

Typesetting and origination by The History Press
Printed and bound in Great Britain by TJ Books Limited, Padstow, Cornwall.

Trees for LYfe

CONTENTS

AUTHOR'S FOREWORD

Vanessa Morgan has called Worcestershire her home for all her life, although being so close to the boundaries of Birmingham she is often mistaken for a Brummie. For as long as she can remember, Vanessa has had an interest in history. Vanessa has worked as a genealogist, gives talks to numerous groups and societies, and has written five books, two on family history and three on nineteenth-century murder and crime.

As the title says, this is a short history of Worcestershire. It touches on many snippets throughout the years and has been written as a taster to encourage the reader to delve deeper into the many aspects of the people and history of the county.

1

WORCESTERSHIRE: EARLY YEARS, GROWTH AND INVASION

So what was Worcestershire like millions of years ago? The Malvern Hills were certainly in existence if nothing else. They are made of rocks 570 million years old. Ancient animals roamed the countryside. Elephants, hippopotamuses and the huge woolly mammoth seemed particularly prevalent around where the River Avon now flows.

There have been at least five ice ages in our history, all of which affected life at the time. The mammoth, like the dinosaurs before, gradually became extinct, but one animal began to develop an intelligence that helped it survive. It found protection by living in caves, and as the ice melted it emerged, finding its way to what is now Worcestershire.

The Flintstones of Worcestershire

Between 600,000 and 10,000 BC the climate fluctuated between cold or hot, and during the warmer spells humans began arriving in the area. They rarely settled in one place for long, travelling from place to place, hunting and picking berries for food. This was a period known as the Third Ice Age, or the Palaeolithic Age, and these early inhabitants were quite recognisable as 'man', showing some form of intelligence. Old Stone Age man was a

The landscape of the Malvern Hills, visible from many parts
of Worcestershire, has been there for many years.

primitive hunter who used simple stone tools. Examples of these
have been found in the Kidderminster area as well as Kemerton,
Bredon Hill, Beckford, Hartlebury Common and along the banks
of where the River Avon now runs. He was sociable, mixing in
small groups and discovering how to fish, hunt animals and collect plants for food.

Before the Severn and the Avon, and other rivers in
Worcestershire, it was the Bytham River that ran across the
Midlands and it was here that the majority of our Worcestershire
ancestors settled. As the ice sheets advanced from East Anglia
to Worcestershire, during what became known as the Anglian
Glaciation, that river disappeared and the inhabitants of these
first settlements were driven away by the ever-increasing cold.

From 10,000 BC the climate began to improve and forests
and mixed woodland once more began to spread across the
county. Man returned and from evidence of his basic tools he
was particularly abundant near Kidderminster. As we enter the

Mesolithic period we find the Middle Stone Age man, who has now begun to develop more intelligence. He used microliths, small tools made out of flint, and small, sharp-edged flints that were used as arrows for hunting and fishing. He was semi-nomadic, moving from site to site, staying just long enough to cultivate small areas and chopping down the trees to make room for basic homes. There is evidence for one of these clearings in the Kidderminster area.

The Neolithic, or New Stone Age, man began to accomplish more and to achieve a more advanced culture. His stone tools were more effective and he started using bone and wood as materials too. He lived a more settled life in small communities. Discoveries of long, rectangular ditched enclosures, known as cursor sites, near Evesham and Eckington show that these people were now clearing larger areas of woodland to make pasture land and to build villages. They used local clay to make pottery, with pieces having been found in Broadway. Polished and ground stone axes have also been found; seven in the north-east of the county, eight in the Severn Valley and three in the Avon Valley and the south-east. These people were also acting in a more civilised way. They had started to bury their dead in grave-like elongated mounds known as long barrows.

Then they discovered how to use bronze and copper.

THE BRONZE AND IRON MAN

During the Bronze Age (2500–750 BC), man discovered the alloy made of copper and tin and began making metal tools. A few have been found scattered around Worcestershire, mainly in the Severn Valley and Bredon Hill areas. An axe was found in Kidderminster.

The Bronze Age man of Worcestershire was a farmer, although evidence suggests he reared cattle more than raised crops. He also discovered a type of cremation. Evidence shows of charred bones being placed in an urn then buried in a barrow or mound. Aerial shots have picked up signs of these around Clent and Holt. In the eighteenth century one site in Clent was excavated by Charles Lyttleton, the President of the Society of Antiquaries, and three urns were found containing cremated remains.

It was now 600 BC and man was discovering how to make tools and weapons using steel and carbon, and mass production was born. Bronze Age weapons have been found at Harvington, Evesham, Defford, Bewdley, Holt, Worcester, Kempsey and Pixham. A system of trackways was also developing across the country. Some of them led to Droitwich, where there is evidence of ancient salt works. Soon the Bronze Age was replaced by the Iron Age.

Iron Age people lived in small villages surrounded by ditches with a fence of some kind. The houses were built in clusters and consisted of a circle of wooden poles with low walls of wattle and daub, a mix of straw and mud and manure. They had thatched, pointed roofs.

The village would contain a primitive well and a place to store grain. Pottery and utensils were used and cloth was woven on looms. The villagers bred pigs, sheep and cows, and their farms had small enclosed fields where they grew crops using iron-tipped ploughs. There was also a rudimentary transport system consisting of rough tracks through the cleared areas of woodland.

Two such sites have been found in Worcestershire. One, excavated at Beckford, contained evidence of the round houses and a number of pits, which it is thought were used for storing grain and burning rubbish. In 1957 aerial photographs of Bewdley

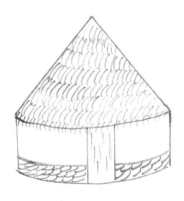

The simple dwelling of Iron Age man.

showed a similar site at Blackstone Rock, which was excavated in the 1970s and '80s. Evidence of a settlement in Worcester is also thought to have existed as pots dating back to 400–100 BC were found in a ditch excavated by the cathedral.

Iron Age man is known for his hill forts. They were built using the natural slopes of a hill and wooden man-made defences erected around the sides. Known as earthworks, there are numerous examples around Worcestershire: British Camp and Midsummer Hill on the Malvern Hills, Wychbury Hill near Hagley, Hanbury Hill near Redditch, Berrow Hill near Martley, Gadbury Camp near Eldersfield, Conderton Camp between Evesham and Tewkesbury, Kemerton Camp on the summit of Bredon Hill, Areley Wood near Bewdley and, the largest of all, Woodbury Hill near Stourport-on-Severn.

On Bredon Hill the summit is crowned by the Bambury Stones. It is thought there may have been just one stone originally but over time the earth's movements caused this to split into pieces. One stone is known as the Elephant Stone, as it resembles what appears to be a kneeling elephant. Over the centuries the stones were known for their so-called healing powers and right up until the twentieth century sickly children were passed through the gaps in the stones in the hope they may be cured.

MASSACRE IN THE IRON AGE

Kemerton Camp was built by the Dobunni tribe and was one in a line of twenty-seven that can be traced a length of almost 50 miles from Clifton Downs, near Bristol, to Bredon Hill. Each fort was built within signalling distance of its neighbour as protection against the Silures tribes in South Wales. The Dobunni were farmers and craftsmen who lived mainly in the south-west of the country, extending into the south of Worcestershire, and are thought to have been a peaceful community.

In the south of England was the war-like Belgae tribe, which originated from Gaul. It took no prisoners and the peaceful

Dobunni tribe were probably an easy target. So was there an attack one fateful day? There are certainly stories of bloody and fierce battles around Bredon Hill, and excavations have revealed a deadly find. At some time the gate to the fort was burnt down and the tribe massacred. Numerous legs, arms and bodies were found lying about surrounded by pottery dating from between 100 BC and AD 100.

In AD 43 people were still living in their individual tribes, with a leader, warriors and workers in their settlements on the hills. But no longer were they the people of the Iron Age; they were now known as the Britons. Then an invader from many miles away appeared.

A New Civilisation Arrives

When the Romans arrived there were four ancient tribes in Worcestershire. In the south were the Dobunnis and in the north the Ordovices. To the west were the Silures and in the centre and the east, the Cornovi. On the whole none of them put up a lot resistance and when their hill settlements were burned they just moved into the valleys. However, one Worcestershire tribe did attempt to put up a fight. Legend has it that the leader of the ancient Britons, Caractacus, placed himself at British Camp on the Malvern Hills to guard against the Roman invasion. However, he expected the Romans to come from the west, but they didn't, and as the ancient Britons didn't use armour, as the Romans did, they were quickly overpowered.

After this initial skirmish the two civilizations lived in peace with each other and eventually become known as the Romano-British civilisation. But there is little evidence of Roman soldiers being based in Worcestershire. It seems to have been a place where civilians lived and worked.

In AD 50 a small Roman settlement grew on high ground by the River Severn. It was named Vertis and is thought to be the beginnings of Worcester as a large quantity of Roman pottery has been found in the southern parts of the city. Slightly downstream, on the banks opposite Kempsey, the remains of timber and oak boards were also found, and this suggests a bridge once stood there. Other parts of the county that show evidence of Roman occupation are in the Kidderminster area. Excavations around Wribbenhall revealed a farmstead and ditched enclosure from the latter part of the Roman occupation. A brooch and coins were found in Habberley and remains of a Roman villa were found in the Wyre Forest. This suggests there was a Roman settlement here for many years.

The Romans are famous for their roads. One of these, the Fosse Way, just misses the main area of Worcestershire, although it passes through two outlying parishes that once belonged to Worcestershire – Blockley and Tredington. The Romans came across the north of the county down Watling Street and Icknield Street, which ran from the Fosse Way in Gloucestershire and passed through Redditch on its way to South Yorkshire.

However, it seems that Droitwich became the main place inhabited by the Romans.

ROMAN SALINAE

The Romans were responsible for the development of Droitwich, which they named Roman Salinae (salt works), and which was one of the first settlements in the area. Evidence of mosaics found in Droitwich suggests a villa belonging to some important Roman person was built there. It appeared that there were eighteen rooms in this house, so it possibly belonged to an administrator in the salt industry of some repute. It burned down in the third century.

Other houses were built on the clifftop at Dodderhill overlooking Droitwich and a large fort was built at Bays Meadow, which is where the parish church, St Andrew's, was later built. Skeletons found on the north-east side of Vines Lane suggest there was a cemetery there.

The Romans certainly took an interest in the existence of salt here as it has been suggested that Droitwich possibly played a part in the formation of the word salary. It derives from the word salarium, which was the allowance of salt given to the soldiers.

At the end of the third century tribes from Northern Europe began to travel across the North Sea, making spasmodic raids along the east coast. The Britons and the Romans defended as best they could but, having been recalled by Rome early in the fifth century, the Romans left England. Without them the Britons were defenceless against the Saxons, who were able to gradually spread across the country as the Britons fled and retreated to Wales and Cornwall.

The Saxons ruled England from 410 until 1066, initially setting up seven individual kingdoms.

THE KINGDOM OF HWICCE AND THE LAND OF MERCIA

In 577 the West Saxon King Cealwin won a great victory over the native Britons at Dyrham in Gloucestershire and the new kingdom of Hwicce was established. It took in what is now modern Gloucestershire, Worcestershire and the western part of Warwickshire and contained a mixture of Saxon and British stock who became known as the Anglo-Saxons.

The Hwicce, also known as the Wiccas, were heathens, and pagan burial sites have been excavated at Upton Snodsbury, Little Hampton and Blockley but they only ruled their kingdom independently for fifty years. In 628 they were defeated at the Battle of Cirencester by the armies of King Penda of Mercia and so became part of the Kingdom of Mercia.

The Hwicce now made their homes in the lower regions below the Severn and by the eighth century it is thought there were about 7,000 families spread over the area. Then, in 670, they settled in Roman Vertis, which gradually began to develop in importance.

AUGUSTINE'S OAK

Christianity had been introduced during the latter period of the Roman supremacy but with the arrival of the Saxons had only spread to parts of the country. In 597 King Ethelbert of Kent had been converted to Christianity by St Augustine, a Roman monk, and the monk was eager to convert the whole country. With the help of King Ethelbert, he arranged a meeting with Saxon dignitaries at a place on the borders of the Hwiccas and other West Saxon communities. The story tells that suspicions were aroused when rumours were heard of Augustine being an arrogant man and that he did not possess the humility expected of a man of God. Therefore the Saxons decided that if he remained seated when they approached, he was not a true religious man. Arriving at the meeting they found him seated underneath an oak tree and when he did not stand up to greet them they turned and returned across the river.

It has never been ascertained exactly where this oak tree was, but tradition has always claimed that it was at Mitre Oak near Hartlebury. The feeling was so strongly held that it was here in 1575 that the bishop and the clergy of Worcester chose to meet Queen Elizabeth on her journey through the county. This would fit in with the suggestion that the group of Saxon dignitaries had crossed the River Severn. This particular oak became so large that a gatekeeper used it to stable his three donkeys. It has gone now but a tree does still stand on the side of the Worcester to Kidderminster road, which is said to be a sapling from the original. This sapling is also now an old tree and is surrounded by an iron fence to protect it from interference.

Rock also has a claim as in Saxon times it was called Ther Ac (the oak). There certainly was an oak tree there at one time but it unfortunately met with a sad end in 1757. Close to this old oak was the toll keeper's house. Being so old, the trunk had become hollow, so when the toll house was being rebuilt the gatekeeper decided to take shelter inside the trunk. It was a cold night so he decided to build a fire inside his temporary accommodation. Whether it was plain stupidity or complete ignorance, his actions were to have devastating consequences. The tree caught alight and within a few hours had been completely destroyed.

THE FIRST CHRISTIAN KING OF WORCESTER

King Penda ruled his kingdom from Tamworth which, following many other successful battles, became the most powerful in the country. He was a pagan and it wasn't until he died in 655 that the whole country became Christian. His son, Paeda, married the daughter of the Christian King Oswy of Northumberland on the condition that he converted to the Christian faith.

In 680 Archbishop Theodore created the See of Mercia, with the Bishop's seat being known as St Peter's, which has long since disappeared. Around the same time, St Mary's Church was built in Worcester and this was later to become the cathedral.

BIRTH OF THE CITY

There are conflicting stories as to how Worcester came into being. The Hwiccas did settle in the old Roman town of Vertis but they also farmed land on the banks of the Severn, which was probably near the remains of Vertis. They named it Wire-cester, the place of wares. Ceaster was, in actual fact, a Roman word meaning settlement or fort. But some say it was also known as Weogoran, the Saxon word for 'people of the winding river'. Taking into account the Ceaster, this can also be translated as 'fort of the Weogorans'.

Worcester soon became the main settlement in the area and before long had become the capital of what was still known as Hwicce. Although it belonged to Mercia, it was still considered a small kingdom in its own right and in 701 was ruled by Penda's third son, King Ethelred. Then it was given a charter by Worfarnis, with its liberties being extended by King Offa of

Mercia (757–795). In 877 walls were built around the perimeter to protect it against the Danes, which showed it was obviously considered an important town.

THE BIRTH OF AN ABBEY

In 701 the third Bishop of Worcester was Egwin, a nephew of the King of Mercia (possibly Ethelred), who travelled around the diocese preaching and baptising. With few churches around at that time, he would have used well-known landmarks or preaching crosses. It happened that one day a swineherd called Eoves saw a vision of the Madonna on the banks of the River Avon and rushed to Bishop Egwin to tell him what he had seen. The bishop immediately asked to be taken to the spot. He gave it his blessings, then founded a monastery there. This was to become Evesham Abbey, the name Evesham deriving from the swineherd's name and the Saxon word 'ham', meaning settlement.

THE LEGEND OF KENELM

Below the Clent Hills in the north of the county is the site of a lost township. Kenelmstowe was an important town in medieval times and attracted many visitors due to its connections with a royal murder, a miracle and its holy spring.

Kenulf, King of Mercia, also known as Coenwulf, was the son of King Offa. When he died in 819 he left one young son, Kenelm, and two older daughters, Quendryda and Burgenhida. Quendryda, the eldest daughter, was entrusted with the guardianship of her young brother but she was jealous that just because he was a boy, he had become king. She was also very ambitious and was determined to be queen. But this could only happen if her brother was dead. Over the next few years the hatred festered until one day she persuaded her lover, Askobert, to murder her brother.

The summer months were spent on the Clent Hills where Kenulf had built a hunting lodge. So when a hunting trip was planned in the forests between the hills and Romsley, known as Cowbach Valley, Askobert had an ideal opportunity. The night before the hunt Kenelm had a dream. In it he climbed a large tree covered in flowers and lanterns. From the top he could see all around his kingdom. Suddenly the tree was being chopped down, and as it fell Kenelm turned into a white dove and flew away. When he told a servant, a wise old woman, about the dream she cried because she knew it meant he was going to die.

The following day as the hunt progressed, Kenelm stopped to rest. As he slept, Askobert went up to him, chopped his head off then buried him under a thorn bush. Quendryda announced that Kenelm had mysteriously disappeared and therefore it was her right to claim the throne. But she was always under the shadow of suspicion. Angry about these suspicions, she decreed that anyone who searched for the prince or even mentioned his name would be beheaded.

Months later the Pope was officiating at St Peter's in Rome when a white dove flew in through the window carrying a scroll in its beak, which it dropped at his feet. The words on the scroll told of Kenelm's body lying under a thorn in Cowbach. Intrigued by the message, the Pope sent word to the Archbishop of Canterbury, who then sent men out from Winchcombe to search the area around Clent. At first they had no idea where to look but were guided to the spot by a shaft of light and the lowing of a milk-white cow. As they lifted the body out of its makeshift grave a spring suddenly gushed from the earth, which, it was discovered, brought good health to anyone who drank from it.

As they returned to Winchcombe with the young boy's body, all the bells began to ring at the abbey and crowds came out shouting, 'He is God's martyr! He is God's martyr!' Asking what all the commotion was about, Quendryda was told that her brother's body had been found and the people were declaring him a martyr. At the time she was reading a book of psalms and caustically replied, 'He is indeed God's martyr, as truly as my eyes

A stone carving depicts
the young King Kenelm
on the walls of St Kenelm's
Church near Romsley.

are resting on this psalter.' With that her eyes fell from her face onto the pages of the open book and she died. No one could be found who was willing to bury her, so her body was thrown into a ditch and devoured by wolves and birds of prey.

The story continued that the young king was buried at the side of his father at the east end of Winchcombe Abbey. When excavations took place in 1815, two stone coffins were indeed found containing the body of an adult and the body of a child.

Kenelmstowe disappeared when the road between Bromsgrove and Dudley was diverted. However, close to the spot on Chapel Lane, Romsley, is St Kenelm's Church. A short walk from the side of the church takes you to the spring, which still exists.

MORE VISITORS FROM OVERSEAS

In the ninth century the coastline of Britain, in particular the east coast, began to witness raids from other invaders – the Danes, more commonly known as the Vikings. During this period the black dragon boats of these intruders floated up the Severn and on more than one occasion reached the shallows of the Diglis, very close to the city walls. At the time the city was poorly defended and the citizens, on seeing these ferocious warriors, fled and hid in the neighbouring woods. Swarming over the walls, the Vikings did what the Vikings did and ransacked the whole town. They took whatever valuables they could find and set buildings on fire. Those who had been unable to hide in the woods were murdered.

One Dane discovered the Sanctus bell in the cathedral and in his eagerness to steal it delayed his return to the boats. He was left behind. When the people of Worcester returned they realised that one Viking on his own was not as fearsome as a group so he was easily captured. Angry at the devastation of their town, they flayed him alive. The man's skin was then tanned and nailed to the doors of the cathedral, where it remained for hundreds of years. A Dr Prattinton of Bewdley once wrote that he remembered as a schoolboy in the 1780s being shown what was supposedly human skin on the inside of the north door of the cathedral.

During renovations in the early 1800s this old door was removed and forgotten but fifty years later Jabez Allies, a Worcester antiquarian, asked to search the cathedral and did find part of an old door on which was a parchment-like piece of material. On having it examined by the Royal College of Surgeons, it was confirmed that it was human skin and the hairs on it were from a person who had light hair.

Following this attack on Worcester, King Alfred held a special court to arrange for its rebuilding and gave half the royal taxes in Worcester for this to be achieved. Alfred's connection to Worcestershire is through his daughter, Aethelflaed, who married Ethelred of Mercia. It was Ethelred who turned some of the towns into well-defended burghs, which were maintained by taxes on the local markets and streets. The first of these was Worcester. New walls were built around the city to replace the earlier ones but they were built further out, therefore producing a much larger area on the inside and also extending the town. The wall was to remain there until the 1600s.

Although Mercia was attacked during this period, there is little evidence of any Viking settlements in Worcestershire. The typical ending of Scandinavian place names are noticeably absent in the towns of Worcestershire. Of course, when the Danes did eventually conquer the eastern part of England an agreement was reached that the country would be divided in half. The Vikings would have one half and the Saxons the other. Worcestershire fell into the Saxon half.

When Alfred died in 899 his son, Edward, went on to conquer all the Danes' land south of the Humber. The country now became 'The Land of the Angles' – in other words, England.

WORCESTERSHIRE, WARWICKSHIRE, GLOUCESTERSHIRE AND WINCHCOMBESHIRE

In 927 Aethelstan, King of Wessex and grandson of Alfred the Great, created the unified Kingdom of England. The country was now split into districts, which became known as shires. Each shire had its own fortified town, known as a burgh. These burghs became the town from which the county acquired its name. Each shire consisted of around 1,200 hides, a hide being the size of a piece of land that was large enough to support a family. Borders of each shire were arranged in a way to make the shires more or less equal for both tax purposes and military purposes. The old Hwiccan kingdom was too large for this purpose, so was divided into four shires – Worcestershire, Warwickshire, Gloucestershire and Winchcombeshire. However, the county of Winchcombeshire was short-lived. By the time of the Domesday Survey in 1086, for some reason not documented, it has disappeared. There are just the three counties we know today and Worcestershire has gained the area south of Evesham.

Many Anglo-Saxon place names have survived. The name Malvern derived from a mixture of Saxon and Welsh using the words Moel, the Saxon word for bare, and the Welsh, Bryn, meaning hill. Bredon combines two words that both, apparently, mean hill – bre and dun. Translated, Eckington, the farm of Ecca's people, incorporates the name of the tribe of Ecca and the Saxon word tun or ton, which can either mean farm or village. Leah or Ley means wood, clearing or glade in woodland, so typical examples here are Beoley, the beekeeper's clearing, and Arley, the wood of the eagle.

A COUNTY TAKES SHAPE

When Worcestershire was created it took into account the estates owned by the Bishop of Worcester, which included pieces of land not attached to the main area. These became known as islands and included the parishes of Shipston-on-Stour, Tredington, Blockley and Dudley.

In those early days part of Halesowen belonged to the Earl of Shrewsbury, so therefore it was initially included in the county of Shropshire. Bewdley was also an anomaly as no one seemed to know if it was in Worcestershire or Shropshire. Not being included in either county, it became a sanctuary for criminals and it wasn't until 1544, after an Act of Parliament made by Thomas Tye, that it became part of Worcestershire.

With Worcester being the seat of an important bishop, it grew quite rapidly during the following 200 years, probably more than any other town in the county. But as trade increased in the tenth century other towns also began to grow. The first to show signs of growth was Bromsgrove, as it is mentioned in ancient documents of 909. Evesham and Pershore's growth were helped by them being monastic estates, plus both having the early beginnings of marketplaces. Tenbury was also growing as it is mentioned as being on a trade route from Pensax.

Droitwich, of course, had already been around for some time. Old charters refer to its salt works being in existence as early as the eighth century. Tolls were being paid by pack horses and carts on its trade routes as early as 740, with destinations as far afield as Northampton and Somerset. On three occasions in the years 836,

884 and 964, grants were made by Mercian rulers for the manufacturing of salt around Droitwich, Hanbury and Himbleton.

ANGLO-SAXON BISHOPS OF WORCESTER

When Christianity eventually arrived in Hwicce, the then Archbishop of Canterbury, Theodore of Tarsus, sent a monk from Whitby called Bosel to act as head of the Diocese of Worcester. Bishop Bosel was also responsible for the founding of the Worcester Royal Grammar School in 685, which is the fifth oldest grammar school in England. It is thought he died a short time after resigning in 691.

In no time Worcester became the centre of the Anglo-Saxon Church and many priests and monks were recruited from its diocese, so great was its reputation. This meant that the Bishops of Worcester also became a very powerful and wealthy authority.

Oswald became the Bishop of Worcester in 961. His parents were Danish and he had been brought up by his uncle Oda, who was the Archbishop of Canterbury. A great advocator of monastic reforms, he founded a number of monasteries that included Pershore Abbey, and in 983 he built a new Worcester cathedral and monastery. All these religious houses dominated the county and brought great power and influence. As well as being Bishop of Worcester, Oswald also became Archbishop of York in 972. Every day during Lent he would wash the feet of the poor and when he died in Worcester in February 992 it was said that miracles took place during his funeral service.

Ealdred became Bishop of Worcester in 1046. His career in the church began as a monk in Winchester and from there he became the Abbot of Tavistock Abbey before moving to Worcester. It is said that he was the bishop who crowned Harold Godwinson following the death of Edward the Confessor. This has never been proved, however it is documented that it was he who crowned William the Conqueror on Christmas Day in 1066. When he left Worcester to become Archbishop of York he suggested his replacement should be Wulfstan, which proved to be the right choice. Ealdred died in York in 1069.

WILLIAM ARRIVES

The Normans arrived in Worcester to find it dominated by Bishop Wulfstan. But despite his Saxon background he did become a strong supporter of William and assisted at the coronation on Christmas Day in 1066. The peaceful life after the arrival of the Normans in Worcestershire was helped by the fact that Bishop Wulstan supported their rules and regulations without question and gave his blessing to both Saxon and Norman alike.

The church owned much of the land in Worcestershire but with William came a new type of aristocrat – the baron and the knight. The most powerful baron to come to Worcester was William's cousin, Urse d'Abitot, whose family had taken the name from a village near Le Havre. Urse was appointed Sheriff of Worcester and immediately began constructing a new castle overlooking the river and close to the cathedral. It was completed in 1069. Made of wood, it was eventually replaced with stone with a tower being added. Many years later Worcester gaol was built in its precincts. Then, between 1829 and 1840 the motte was levelled and now only a small amount of stonework survives in the wall of King's School.

Other Norman castles appeared over Worcestershire. Ansculf de Picquigny built Dudley Castle, which became the home of his son William Fitz Ansculf, and Robert Despenser built Elmley Castle. There are a few remnants left around the county of other castles with Norman mottes and earthworks at Clifton-on-Teme and Tenbury Wells.

The Lechmere family originated in the Low Countries, possibly near to Utrecht, and were given land at Hanley Swan by William. Here they built Rhydd Court, where the family remained until 1915. The property was then given to the Red Cross for war use and the family moved to another of their houses, Severn End, which had been built in the seventeenth century. After the First World War Rhydd Court was sold and turned into a school. However, following accusations of sexual abuse and cruelty it was closed and it is now a residential home for autistic adults.

The Berkeley family history can be traced back further than the Normans to a Viking named Hardinge, who was a younger son of the King of Denmark and who settled in Bristol. His son, Robert, married the niece of William I, so theoretically became a Norman. A branch of the family settled in Worcestershire and became wealthy clothiers and bankers. Rowland Berkeley bought the Spetchley Park estate in 1605, and it is still owned by the family. His son, William, acquired Cotheridge Court in 1615 and his family remained there until the Second Word War, when rising costs forced the then owner to sell and move to the Isle of Wight. The house is now luxury apartments.

The Normans built many new churches and monasteries. Great Malvern Priory was built in 1085 by Uldwyn and became home to thirty monks. Uldwyn, also known as Aldwin, was a Benedict monk at Worcester Priory who was preparing to undertake a pilgrimage. Conflicting stories tell that he was planning to go to Jerusalem, whereas others say that he wanted to go to Rome to receive the Pope's blessing. Whichever is true, the Bishop intervened and said he would do more good founding a monastery. At the time Malvern was a remote region surrounded by forest that had been occupied by St Werstan, a monk who, having fled from the Danes, lived as a hermit. He had eventually been found by the Danes and killed, with a shrine being erected close to the spot. It was here that Aldwin chose for his monastery.

Little Malvern Priory was founded much later, supposedly about 1171, it is said by two brothers from Worcester, Joselin and Edred, who had wanted to live secluded lives in the forest. However, it is believed a priory dating back to earlier in the twelfth century did exist, prior to the arrival of Joselin and Edred.

The Normans also transformed Pershore Abbey, which had been founded in 689, into a Benedictine abbey. Also the religious houses of Worcester and Evesham. The Cistercian abbey at Bordesley was built in 1138 on land given to them by Waleran de Beaumont, 1st Earl of Worcester. The Cluniac Priory of St James, Dudley, was built in around 1160.

WULFSTAN, THE LAST ANGLO-SAXON BISHOP

When William arrived, Bishop Wulfstan was head of the diocese of Worcester.

From the time of Alfred the Great, the Diocese of Worcester had been one of the most important dioceses in the country and the bishops of Worcester were considered important advisors to the king in both spiritual and government issues. So Wulfstan had been close to both Edward the Confessor and King Harold. In fact, he had been one of Harold's close confidants.

He was born in Long Itchington in Warwickshire in 1008 and was encouraged by his parents to become a priest – his mother had become a nun and his father a monk – so he went to study in the monasteries of Evesham and Peterborough. After his studies he became a clerk at Worcester before serving as treasurer and then prior. When Ealdred became Archbishop of York and resigned his post in Worcester, he suggested Wulfstan as his successor. The consecration took place on 8 September 1062.

A social reformer, Wulfstan worked hard to reduce the sufferings of the poor, although he struggled at times to convince people to make the changes from the old regime to a new one. Under his care a large-scale rebuilding of Worcester Cathedral took place, as well as many other churches in Worcestershire.

At the start of his reign, William began to replace Anglo-Saxon bishops with his own men and Wulfstan was ordered to Westminster, where he was asked to surrender his bishop's ring and staff. He placed them both on the tomb of Edward the Confessor, saying he would only surrender them to the person he had received them from. The legend tells that once the items were placed on the tomb no one was able to move them apart from

Wulfstan himself. Because of this William allowed him to remain as Bishop of Worcester.

Another legend tells of Wulfstan's hatred of long hair and that he always carried a sharp knife with him so that when an individual who had long hair bent before him he would take out the knife and cut off a piece of the man's hair. He would then tell the individual that by way of penance he was to cut the rest off in the same way.

In 1084 he began building a new cathedral to replace the one St Oswald had built. Norman builders and architects were brought over from Normandy as they were considered far superior to local people. Certainly when the cathedral was completed in 1089 it was said to be the most outstanding in England.

Wulfstan died on 20 January 1095, having witnessed the start of the Norman reign. He was canonised in 1203.

Worcester Cathedral.

THE VICAR'S SALARY

The people of Norman England became divided between lords of the manor, landowners, freemen, knights and commoners. The county was made up of 1,200 hides, of which the church owned 786 and the remainder were owned by various laymen. The term hide was altered in Norman times to refer to a piece of land farmed by a peasant, and its dimensions have not really been ascertained. By the twelfth and thirteenth centuries it appears to have amounted to around 120 acres but is thought to have been a much smaller unit previously.

Life around most parts of the county revolved around the monasteries and churches. One tenth of produce from the land within a parish had to be given to the church. Tithes were introduced as a way of taxing inhabitants in order to provide for the maintenance of the parish church and the incumbent. The word derives from an old English word, Teogotha, meaning one tenth.

Some churchmen were very pedantic about receiving one tenth of everything and in the early nineteenth century one such vicar paid the price for this. In 1806 landowners in the village of Oddingley were so fed up with the Rev. George Parker demanding his one tenth that they actually hired a 'hit man' to shoot him!

The first documentation of the collection of tithes was between 926 and 930 when King Edgar determined that a nobleman was to pay one third of the tenth to his church and two thirds to the minister. Once the parish boundaries were determined, tithes were only paid to the church and it was the clergy's responsibility to give a proportion to the poor. A reeve was appointed to collect tithes and barns were built for storing the collections of corn and hay. They became known as tithe barns and some were quite impressive buildings, made of stone and looking very much like miniature churches. Two still remain in Worcestershire at Middle Lyttleton and Bredon. Both are run by the National Trust.

The 1836 Tithe Act introduced a rent charge to replace tithes, which itself was abolished in 1936 and the clergy were then given salaries.

COUNTING THE POPULATION

At the time of the Domesday survey in 1086, Worcestershire was said to be divided between the church estates, fourteen French noblemen and twenty-six knights.

Commoners were split up as villeins/villani or peasants (villagers), bordars/bordarii or cottars (smallholders) or slaves/serfs (servants). Villagers would hold anything from a few strips of land to up to 30 acres of common fields within the manor for their own use. They paid for this by working the lord's land for a certain number of days, probably one or two, per week and also gave a percentage of their produce. There were also laws and regulations they were bound by. They couldn't marry without permission or pass their land to their children. Bordars held smaller amounts of land, anything from just a small patch to around 5 acres, and also had feudal duties too. The lowest group were the serfs. They owned no land at all and only worked for the lord on his land.

The total count in Worcestershire in 1086 appears to be 1,666 villeins, which included smiths and millers, and 1,821 bordars with 15 per cent of the overall total being serfs and bondswomen (ancillae). There were also beekeepers, millers, huntsmen, swineherds, cowmen and dairymaids. And there were priests, reeves and beadles and millers listed.

The survey suggests that the poorest village in Worcestershire was Little Witley as it only had one priest and two smallholders with one plough. Part of their tax was paid in honey. Among other towns listed is Bromsgrove containing three hundred hides with a steward, bailiff, priest, twenty villeins and ninety-two bordars. Chaddesley Corbett had thirty-three villeins, twenty bordars, two priests, twenty-five ploughs and eight serfs. Droitwich was split between sixty-eight manors and estates, and Kidderminster was stated as being a whole manor of waste. The county's population was denser in the south-east.

One of the officials who compiled the entries for Worcestershire was Roeland de Trokemardune. His estate was in Throckmorton, which, of Saxon origins, means 'farm by a drain, marsh or pond'.

The Throckmorton family gradually prospered and became an important one in Worcestershire. By the early 1400s Thomas de Throckermerton was a Knight of the Shire and represented the county in the king's Parliament. The family would go on and prosper even more but not in Worcestershire. John, Thomas's son, married Eleanor Spinney, the heiress of Coughton in Warwickshire, and founded the family who still live at Coughton Court today.

THE HUNDREDS

The hundreds were originally introduced around 613 when it had been decided to divide the kingdom into shires and counties and set up a regular court system. The shires had then been divided into hundreds, and the hundreds into tythings. A hundred was decided by the amount of land that would be sufficient to hold 100 homes with enough land to sustain that household. A tything was a tenth of the hundred. Worcestershire was originally divided into twelve hundreds. Every hundred had its own court and offices, and a designated building was provided where officials could meet regularly to discuss legal, criminal and social matters within their hundred. However, the court was often held at some ancient site where a stone or large tree was prominent. Doddingtree was a good example of this old ritual.

The Church was very much in control of the hundreds. The bishop and monks in Worcester owned three hundreds around the city, which took the name Oswaldslow. Two in the Pershore district were owned by the Church of Westminster, while the parishes of Evesham and Pershore owned another two. The remaining five were the hundreds of Doddingtree, in the western part of the county; Esch, the area around Feckenham; Clent, the north-west of the county; Came, which included the parishes of Bromsgrove and Northfield, and finally Cresselaw, which took in the north-east of the county.

With the arrival of the Normans the system was modernised and the number of 'hundreds' in Worcestershire decreased to five, with only Oswaldslow and Doddingtree keeping their old, ancient names. The church lands of Westminster simply became the Hundred of Pershore. Evesham became Blackenhurst and Came, Clent and Esch formed the Halfshire Hundred.

The Blackenhurst Hundred was situated in the south-east of the county and included the parishes around Evesham and the Lenches. Doddingtree was on the western side and took in Bewdley, Clifton upon Teme, Rock and Shrawley. The Bromsgrove, Droitwich, Feckenham, Tardebigge, King's Norton, Kidderminster and Stourbridge areas belonged to the Halfshire, while Shipton upon Stour, Sedgeberrow and Teddington were in the Oldwaldeslow hundred. In the southern part of the county was the Pershore Hundred with the parishes of Broadway, Peopleton, Strensham, Powick and Malvern.

It also became law that each hundred would have to pay tax to the king, so each county had a shire-reeve (sheriff) who would collect the taxes from each hundred in his county.

A PLAYGROUND FOR ROYALTY

A royal prerogative forest law came into operation that was designed to protect venison, deer and wild boar, and the woods that sustained them. Certain areas became known as royal hunting grounds, or royal forests, and were reserved for the use of the monarch and other nobility who had made arrangements with the king to do so. The forests designated in Worcestershire were Feckenham Forest, Wyre Forest, Horewell Forest and Malvern Chase, which covered a large area of Worcestershire. Feckenham Forest stretched between Stone, Staffordshire, in the north, Evesham in the south, Worcester in the west and Alcester (just over the border into Warwickshire) in the east, also taking in the Clent and Lickey Hills. Wyre Forest was in the north-west around Kidderminster and Bewdley, while Horewell Forest covered Strensham in the south across to Pershore. Malvern Chase, which had originally formed part of the Forest of Dean, stretched between the River Severn and the Malvern hills, taking in Hanley Castle, Upton upon Severn, Castlemorton, Berrow and Malvern and over the border to Colwall in Herefordshire.

At first William planned to move people out of these areas and have their homes destroyed. But this almost caused an uprising so a law was brought in allowing people to continue to live in these forests. A team of officials was then employed to keep guard and prevent poaching. The law stated that an eye would be removed if someone was found disturbing the king's deer and that a death sentence would be imposed upon anyone killing one of the king's deer. Fines were later introduced to replace these harsh sentences. There would also be fines if anyone was found clearing a piece of land within a forest. Nevertheless, parts of the forest land were cleared over the ensuing centuries. Each forest had a warden and foresters who looked after separate areas, and as foresters weren't well paid they could easily be bribed.

Special courts were established to keep law and order in the forest. One of these was in the village of Feckenham and on the south-west side of the church today can be found remains of the ditch that surrounded the gaol. There was also a royal hunting lodge in Feckenham.

A WOOLLY JUMPER AND A FINE VINTAGE

As well as its abundance of forests, Worcestershire had plenty of open grazing land and under the Normans was known as the capital of the wool industry. This had first developed in Roman times and by the eleventh century had become England's chief export, with wool from Worcestershire being in great demand. Here the sheep grazed in meadows filled with luscious grass and so produced wool of great quality.

The Romans had also introduced winemaking to Britain but it was the Normans who continued the practice and there are still traces of ancient vineyards in Worcestershire today. In Great Hampton there is a place called Vineyard Hill, although this is believed to have been established later than Norman times. In South Littleton there is Vineyard Orchard, in Evesham a street named Vine Street, and in Droitwich there is an area known as The Vines. A rector's garden in Fladbury is supposedly the site of a vineyard that was cultivated in Henry II's time.

A LORD GOES TO THE CRUSADES

The crusades took place between 1095 and 1291 and saw many members of the nobility leaving England to fight against the Saracens (the medieval name for Muslims) in the Holy Land. Among these was Sir John Attwood. The Attwood family were the lords of the manor of Wolverley, whose original name was du Bois. They had been Knights of Brittany and when they arrived in England after the Battle of Hastings they changed their name to Attwood.

Before leaving for the crusades, Sir John Attwood broke his ring in half. Keeping one half, he gave the other half to his wife as a sign of his love. While on crusade he was captured and imprisoned. He was away so long it was presumed he had been killed, so eventually his wife decided to marry again. On the morning of the wedding a milkmaid was out looking for a lost cow. She was accompanied by the family dog, who suddenly ran off, barking loudly. Following it, she found a man asleep under a hedge wearing iron shackles. He was starving, dirty and scruffy. At first she thought he was an escaped vagrant but Sir John's dog began whimpering and lay at the man's side as if he knew him. The maid rushed back to her mistress, who followed the girl back to the spot. On seeing Lady Attwood, the vagrant began talking to her in an intimate way. She stepped back, horrified – then he produced his half of the ring.

Sir John told a story of being locked in a dungeon for longer than he could remember until one night, before falling asleep, he fervently prayed to one day return home. He was woken by the sound of a dog barking and discovered he was home.

At the time when John Noakes was writing his books on Worcestershire he wrote that Sir John's shackles were still kept at Wolverley Court and the meadow in which he was found had been named Knight's Meadow.

A KING AND AN EMPRESS

In 1138 a nineteen-year conflict began between King Stephen and the Empress Matilda.

King Henry I had two children, Matilda and William. William died young when a ship he was travelling on sank off the French coast and he drowned. So Henry now made his court swear their allegiance to Matilda, as their future queen. However, when Henry died, his nephew, Stephen du Bois, announced that Henry had changed his mind on his death bed and had proclaimed Stephen as his successor. He therefore claimed the throne with the backing of the church, who preferred to have a king rather than a queen. Stephen reigned for three years but during this time Matilda raised an army and the war known as The Anarchy began.

Robert, the 1st Earl of Gloucester, was Henry's illegitimate son and therefore, as Matilda's half-brother, took her side. So, with its close proximity to Gloucestershire, Worcestershire became embroiled in the hostilities. It certainly would have been in Stephen's interests to occupy Worcestershire, so it was probably for this reason that he attacked Dudley Castle. His attempt failed as he found it strongly protected and impregnable, so he contented himself by ransacking the surrounding countryside.

The following year he visited Worcester, where one of his war-lords and close ally, Waleran de Beaumont, lived. And to keep him on side, Stephen granted Waleran the lordship of Worcester.

In November 1140 Matilda was in Gloucester and it became known she was making plans to attack Worcester. As the armies prepared to attack, the citizens hid in the cathedral. Monks tolled the bells and carried the relics of St Oswald out in front of the cathedral as the enemy charged through the city gates. They burned and looted the city, stole the livestock and took prisoners as ransom. Despite surrounding houses being destroyed, the castle remained undamaged.

Worcester then came under the control of Matilda's army, and William Beauchamp, the grandson of Urse d'Abitot, who had been made Sheriff of Gloucester, entered Worcester and took charge of Worcester Castle. Waleran then sided with Matilda and defended Worcester against Stephen. Other supporters now changed sides and in 1141 Stephen was captured and held prisoner. But one of Matilda's supporters had also been captured, so she had no option but to trade the two prisoners. Following this Stephen decided to avenge those who had changed sides, and this time Worcester went up in flames at his hands.

In 1150 Worcester was retaken by Stephen and this time he had no difficulty entering the city from the north as for some reason no defences were in place on this side. The war continued for another three years until eventually in 1153 Stephen agreed that Matilda's heir would succeed him and peace came.

2

THE HOUSE OF PLANTAGENET

That heir was Henry II, who was Matilda's son by her second husband, Geoffrey Plantagenet, Count of Anjou. So when he came to the throne in 1154 a new royal dynasty began.

In 1158, Henry held a Royal Council in Worcester at Easter, and in 1189 his son, Richard I, gave Worcester its first Royal Charter.

It was during Henry's reign that the Court of Assizes came into being. The courts were grouped into circuits and judges from the high court would travel around these circuits holding sessions every six months. Worcestershire was placed in the Oxford circuit.

Cruck houses can still be found in Worcestershire,
such as this one in Ombersley.

The majority of the rural population at this time were peasants, whose lives consisted of farming small pieces of land. Their homes were very basic timber dwellings measuring about 37ft long and known as cruck houses. At one end there was an upper room, while the rest of the lower room was open to the roof and heated by one hearth. People and animals lived together, albeit at different ends of the building.

The population was growing and the pressure on the land was getting intense, with more people wanting to farm the land available. Certain feudal regulations were lifted and tenants were allowed to break away from the feudal systems and move to the towns. So during the next three centuries many new towns came into existence, with others being expanded. It may seem surprising but the term 'town air breaths free' was a common expression.

The growth of a town was helped to a certain degree by being granted a market, and settlements that had grown around abbeys also prospered. When Pershore established its marketplace, a series of streets quickly spread out from it. In Dudley the small street that had appeared around the foot of the hill by the castle gradually expanded. In 1239 the Bishop of Worcester granted a market to a small settlement in the northeast of the county and Alvechurch soon began to grow into a small town. The Abbot of Hales developed Halesowen when it was granted its market fair in 1220.

Old cottages of a bygone age in Halesowen.

In Evesham the small settlement around the abbey spread out towards the north, becoming known as Bengeworth. Bewdley developed in the parish of Ribbesford during the late thirteenth century and gradually expanded over the following years. Ribbesford had already caught the eye of the Normans, who were so impressed with the picturesque area they had named it Beaulieu (beautiful place).

Industry also began to grow. Kidderminster was making broad cloth as early as 1332. Dudley had its nailers by the fifteenth century. Meanwhile, Droitwich was still a main supplier of salt, a vital commodity as both a condiment and a preserver of meats. Evesham was developing into a fruit-growing area, with many smallholdings springing up, whereas the Teme valley was becoming known for its hops.

As such a large amount of property was owned by the church in Worcestershire, noble families were small in number. One such family was the Beauchamps of Elmley Castle, who owned land in more than fifty manors throughout Worcestershire. William Beauchamp married the heiress of the Earl of Warwick in the mid-thirteenth century, so his son inherited both titles and this made them a high-ranking family. By the late-thirteenth century knights had become more than just professional soldiers on horseback; they were now also administrators and justices of the peace.

A Pious Bishop and a Not So Pious Prior

Roger, Bishop of Worcester, was the son of the 1st Earl of Gloucester, the illegitimate son of Henry I. This also made him Henry II's cousin. They had grown up together and these royal connections must certainly have helped Roger's career. He became Bishop of Worcester on the advice of Thomas Beckett and was ordained in August 1163. Roger was a great supporter of Beckett and loyal to him until the end, attempting to intervene in his cousin's arguments with the archbishop over the benefits and power that the church held. He spent time in exile with Beckett but had reconciled with his cousin before he died in 1179.

Before becoming the prior of Evesham in 1191, Roger Norrey had enjoyed a life of immense luxury. He had first been a monk at Christ Church, Canterbury, before becoming its prior. He was actually convicted of misconduct while in Canterbury and moved on to Evesham. Here he still continued his wicked ways. Often seen drunk and disorderly, he squandered much of the rents from church land on debauchery and kept all the tithes while his monks went hungry and were forced to beg for food. Eventually he was deposed in 1213.

King John of Worcestershire

King John visited Worcester Cathedral regularly, especially at Christmas and Easter, and took particular interest in Wulfstan's tomb. He made eleven visits in total, his first as king being Easter 1200.

These visits to the cathedral gave it a social standing and in 1202 he helped with the rebuilding of Edgar's Gate following a fire. He also reduced the cathedral's taxes when he discovered they had been forced to melt down the gold on a shrine to St Wulfstan, after having been fined 300 marks during the Barons' War. But his interest wasn't just reserved for Worcester; other parts of Worcestershire benefited from his generosity. In 1207 he gave Cleeve Prior and Lindridge their independence from the Hundred Court so they could administer their own justice.

King John also considered Worcestershire to have the best hunting ground. He used a hunting lodge in Feckenham, but also hunted in the Wyre Forest and in order to be close to Malvern Chase he built Hanley Castle, staying there on many occasions.

WHEN THE 'OLD' PALACE WAS 'NEW'

During King John's reign the Old Palace of Worcester was built by Bishop Mauger and became the official residence of the Bishops of Worcester. During its history it has been visited by Elizabeth I, James II and George III. It was used by the war council during the Civil War and now houses the deanery of Worcester Cathedral.

UPRISING IN THE RANKS OF NOBILITY

Known as the First Barons' War, this uprising took place between 1215 and 1216. It was caused by a quarrel between King John and a group of barons led by Robert Fitzwalter. John had lost territory in Normandy and needed money to raise an army, so he increased the taxes on the nobility. Angry at this, certain barons in the north raised an army. The result was the signing of the Magna Carta.

This skirmish hardly touched Worcestershire, apart from Ranulph, Earl of Chester, attacking Worcester, ransacking the cathedral and storming the castle. William Marshall, the governor of Worcester and son of the Earl of Pembroke, escaped. The prior of Worcester was later fined for hiding rebels and forced to melt down treasures in order to pay the fine. The City of Worcester was also fined £100 for its role.

A CUNNING DISGUISE

King John died in Newark in 1216 but left a written command that he was to be buried in Worcester Cathedral between Worcester's two saints, Oswald and Wulstan. A local legend says that he also ordered that his royal robes were to be covered with a monk's habit and the cowl was to be pulled down over his face. He thought that at the Resurrection his disguise, and being in the company of the two saints, would enable him to evade the vigilance of the gatekeepers of heaven. Many hundreds of years later, in the eighteenth century, his tomb in the choir was opened. The king's remains were still wrapped in an embroidered robe but with the monk's cowl covering the skull. Made of Purbeck marble, the tomb is the oldest royal effigy in England and is said to be a very good likeness of King John.

THE JEWISH POPULATION OF WORCESTERSHIRE

In the late twelfth century a small community of Jews settled in the Copenhagen Street district of Worcester and William de Blois, the Bishop of Worcester, imposed strict rules. They were not allowed to work with Christians and they had to wear white square badges as identification. In 1240 Henry III summoned all prominent Jewish people to Worcester to have their wealth assessed for tax purposes and in the lead-up to the Second Barons' War they were attacked by rebel barons, led by Earl Robert Ferrers and Henry de Montfort. By 1275 all Jews still living in Worcester were banished to Hereford.

THE NOBLE BARONS REVOLT AGAIN

Worcestershire was in the midst of the Second Barons' War. A baronial force attacked Worcester in 1263 and, after a series of assaults, took hold of the city. In the south of the country, the Battle of Lewes took place the following year and King Henry III was taken prisoner. The Earl of Leicester, Simon de Montford, was then made head of state. But when the king's army regained possession of Worcester it was now in an excellent position. With Gloucester and Monmouth also being held in the king's name it maintained a hold along the Severn, which included its bridges and boats. Simon was forced to retreat from Hereford and his son, also Simon, went to his mother's castle in Kenilworth to rest his men.

On 2 August 1265 Prince Edward moved from Worcester towards Kenilworth, therefore cutting off communication between father and son. At around the same time, Simon crossed the Severn at Kempsey and, after a two-and-a-half day march, arrived in Evesham with the intention of moving on to join his son in Kenilworth. Still holding King Henry III prisoner, he and his army gathered at Harvington Hall and blocked the road to Evesham.

Knowing Simon's movements, Prince Edward marched from Kenilworth towards Evesham carrying banners he had captured at Kenilworth. Seeing them, the lookouts thought it was young Simon de Montford and his men returning, so they did not advance. When the enemy dropped the Kenilworth banners and held their own aloft it was too late. As the sun began to rise on 4 August 1265, Simon found himself surrounded on the loop in the River Avon near Evesham. His eldest son, Henry, told him to escape but he refused, saying he was happy to die in battle. One friend stood by his side: Walter de Cantelupe, the Bishop of Worcester, who, after giving the troops plenary absolution, also gave them reassurance to face their enemy.

The two armies met in a large field outside Evesham during the afternoon, with the fighting continuing until night-time. It was a fierce battle with both sides fighting desperately in raging thunderstorms, but for Simon it was a hopeless situation and he was vastly outnumbered. The king, wearing an ordinary suit of armour, was still a prisoner and Simon kept him close at hand. At one point Henry was wounded and was just about to be killed when he called out – 'I am Henry of Winchester, your king, kill me not.'

Gradually the battle appeared to be coming to an end and although de Montford's horse had been killed, he continued to fight on foot. Standing alone in defiance, he wielded his great two-handed sword and refused to give in. Eventually he was struck from behind and killed.

Simon's body was badly mutilated, with his head and hands chopped off and sent to the wife of the victor, Baron Roger

Mortimer, at Worcester Castle. His body was taken to Evesham Abbey, where he and his son, Henry, who had died early in the battle, were buried together by the monks.

A Close Call in Kidderminster

Whether it was before the Barons' War or after is not really known but at one time Henry III was staying in Kidderminster as a guest of John Biset, who was lord of the manor of Wolverhampton. His house was situated between Dudley Street and Orchard Street, where the ring road is now, and later became a carpet factory. Another guest, only known as Margaret, heard a muffled creeping sound during the night. Investigating, she discovered a man making his way to the king's room. She raised the alarm, the would-be assassin was caught, and the king was saved.

A Wedding at the Cathedral

When William the Conqueror settled in England he had made no attempt to extend his lands into Wales. All he did was build a line of castles to defend the borders of Wales and England. In the thirteenth century Llewelyn ap Gruffydd, grandson of Llewelyn the Great, was Prince of Wales. In order to set up an alliance with Wales, Simon de Montford had arranged a marriage between his daughter, Eleanor, and Prince Llewellyn. But following her father's death, she and her mother had fled to France, where they stayed for ten years.

In 1275, in order to annoy Edward I, Llewellyn renewed his wedding plans and Eleanor made her way back to England. On her return she was captured by Edward I and imprisoned in Windsor Castle. There now followed a year of disputes and arguments until Llewelyn paid homage to Edward and agreed for some of his lands to be taken in return for Eleanor. Their wedding took place at Worcester Cathedral on 13 October 1278 and is said to have been an extremely lavish affair, with a guest list that included Edward I and Alexander III of Scotland. The wedding feast was paid for by Edward himself.

NEIGHBOURS ARGUE OVER BOUNDARY RIGHTS

As mentioned before, there are two ancient forts on the Malvern Hills: the Herefordshire Beacon, which is a triple entrenchment and usually known as British Camp, and Midsummer Hill. Then, along the whole length of the hills, is what is known as Red Earl's Dyke, which marks the boundary between Worcestershire and Herefordshire. In March 1278 this boundary was the subject of a lawsuit between neighbours regarding forest rights.

Thomas De Catelupe, Bishop of Hereford, brought a case against Gilbert de Clare, the Earl of Gloucester and feudal lord of Upton upon Severn and Malvern Chase. Gilbert was also known as the Red Earl, either because of his fiery temper or the colour of his hair, or of course both.

When the bishop won the case, the earl decided to get his own back. He dug a ditch and built a palisade along the top of the hills marking the boundary between the two estates. His was on the east, while the bishop's, which was smaller, was on the west. The fence was made in such a way that the bishop's deer could, and did, jump over it and land down in the earl's land. However, because of the height on the earl's side, they couldn't jump back.

But perhaps the bishop had the last laugh in the end. Today the earl's deer have long since disappeared but it is said the deer that wander the park at Eastnor Castle, over the border, are descendants of the bishop's deer.

ABBOT AND SCOUNDREL

For some reason, when it was founded, the Abbot of Westminster was made the benefactor of Great Malvern Priory for an unspecified time. This was to cause a great legal battle in the thirteenth century.

In 1279 William de Ledbury became prior of Malvern. He was quite a scoundrel and was known to have at least twenty mistresses. While the community was starving, he was spending extravagant amounts on keeping his mistresses happy. The priory, of course, was in the Diocese of Worcester, so Bishop Giffard intervened. In September 1282 Ledbury was replaced by William de Wykewane and, as was the custom, was sent to receive his blessing by the Abbot of Westminster. But instead of being blessed he was thrown into prison.

The Abbot of Westminster said Bishop Giffard had no right to install a new abbot in Malvern and lengthy arguments ensued. Nine months later the problem had still not been resolved. The monks of Malvern had been excommunicated with their pensions and belongings taken away from them, and Wykewane was still in gaol.

Eventually both King Edward I and the Pope became involved, and the Bishop of Worcester and the Abbot of Westminster were ordered to appear before the royal court. Gifford was now shown the documents that proved Malvern belonged to the Abbot of Westminster. With that, the matter was closed and Ledbury was reinstated.

BLACK DEATH

In 1348 the Black Death arrived on the English south coast and within a year it had reached Worcestershire. Death rates across the county differed considerably. In some parts they were as high as 80 per cent, in others as low as 19 per cent. Corn was rotting in the fields as there were not enough people to reap it, and with a lack of herdsmen, cattle and sheep were roaming freely over the countryside. In Worcestershire whole villages disappeared when their entire population died.

But out of the bad came the good. Food prices fell as there were fewer people to be fed. This gave the poor a boost, and with fewer people looking for work, wages also rose for those who could work. When wealthy landowners found themselves in difficulties they allowed their peasants to buy their freedom, thus giving a boost to their finances, and slaves were freed so money could be saved by not having to feed them. Many landowners also moved from agriculture to sheep farming or sold parts of their estates. Suddenly some who had been classed as more lowly landowners found themselves labelled as country squires. And with peasants no longer being tied to one lord they could work for another, for a better wage. Or they could move to the towns and a new career.

The plague also stopped renovation work being carried out on Worcester Cathedral. Numerous clergy died and on 10 December 1361, Brian, the Bishop of Worcester and Chancellor of England, died of the plague.

A Lady Scorned

In the early 1400s the Welsh Revolt took place. Led by Owain Glyndwr, it was a fight for independence against Henry IV and, showing his support, the French king, Charles VI, sent a troop from the French army to assist Owain. They landed at Milford Haven in 1404.

On their march towards Worcester they camped up on Woodbury Hill just south of Witley. For eight days, apart from a few jousts and skirmishes, the two armies just watched each other and waited. Then one morning as the sun rose the English discovered their opponents had just disappeared.

A story does tell that during those eight days a French captain, Jean de Hangest, was captured and taken to Wichenford Court, the home of Lord Washbourne. It is thought he was a nobleman of the Bourbon dynasty, French royalty descended from the youngest son of Louis IX, Lord Bourbon. Unfortunately he was to meet a grisly end. Lady Washbourne was immediately attracted to the French captain but when he showed no interest in her, or her advances, she stabbed him to death.

The Dovecote
that belonged to
Wichenford Court,
now owned by the
National Trust.

THE TAILOR AND THE PRINCE

In 1409 a tailor of Evesham, John Badby, refused to take the consecrated wafer at communion, saying it wasn't the body of Christ. He was therefore taken to Smithfield to be burned as a heretic. Just as he was being chained to a barrel with the faggots piled around him, Prince Henry (later Henry V) arrived. He stopped the twelve torch bearers and began talking to John. Then he asked the prior of St Bartholomew's to offer John the sacrament. When the tailor refused the barrel was put over him, but as it was about to be set on fire the prince once again intervened. He ordered them to remove it while once more he tried to persuade the tailor to take the sacrament. John still refused to forsake his heresy, even though the prince offered him a pension out of the King's Treasury. Eventually the prince left defeated, and the burning took place.

THE LEGEND OF BLACKSTONE ROCK

In meadows close to Bewdley there is a steep escarpment over-looking the Severn and in the rock face are a number of caves. In medieval times a young girl named Alice was to marry Sir Harry Wade of Birmingham. On her way to the wedding she was snatched by a young man on horseback. Pursued by her husband-to-be and others of the wedding party, the young man panicked. He threw Alice into the River Rea at Deritend and escaped into Worcestershire, heading for the safety of Bewdley. Unfortunately Alice drowned and ironically Sir Harry, who was inconsolable, also made his way to Bewdley. He became a hermit and lived in the caves of Blackstone Rock, spending his time in religious pursuits and taking confessionals.

The years progressed until one day a middle-aged man arrived at the caves wanting to make a confession. He said that when he was a young man he had fallen in love but was too shy to approach the young girl. When he found she was to be married, in desperation he had snatched her on her wedding day. On hearing this, Harry flew into a rage, grabbed the man and threw him off the cliff into the river below.

THE WAR OF THE ROSES

Although the War of the Roses lasted thirty years, Worcestershire did not become involved and no battles took place in the county. Life continued as normal for the folk of Worcestershire. However, because Richard, Duke of York, held estates in Bewdley the people there did show their support to both him and his son, who later became Edward IV. For their support, the town became a borough in 1472. Six years later, it was appointed Edward's seat for Wales and the Marches (the strip of land between Wales and Worcestershire).

Only one other town was affected by the War of the Roses and that was Grafton, near Bromsgrove. The manor was owned by the Stafford family and Sir Humphrey Stafford fought with Henry VI's army at Sevenoaks, where he was killed. His nephew, also called Humphrey, inherited the estate and fought with Richard III at the Battle of Bosworth, where he was captured. At first he was pardoned but when he continued to oppose the king (then Henry VII), he was arrested and executed at Tyburn. The estate was then confiscated and given to Sir Gilbert Talbot. The Talbot family then remained at Grafton until the 1930s.

William Sheldon of Beoley Manor fought on the Yorkshire side in the war and after the Battle of Bosworth also had his lands confiscated by Henry VII, although they were returned some years later.

John Sutton, the first Baron Dudley, started on the side of the House of Lancaster but changed his allegiance to Yorkshire. He was King's Counsellor to Henry VI and one of his favourite companions. At the Battle of St Albans in 1455 he was taken prisoner with Henry VI but in 1461, after the Battle of Towton, he changed sides.

Rumour has it that it was Sir John Savage of Elmley who put the crown on Henry Tudor's head rather than Stanley, Earl of Derby.

3

THE TUDOR ERA

By the 1500s cloth making was the staple industry in most of the main towns of Worcestershire such as Bromsgrove, Kidderminster, Droitwich, Evesham and Worcester. In Worcestershire 8,000 people were employed in the wool trade, which included half the population of Worcester. The new king made every effort to revive trade and successfully arranged new export deals. He also invited Flemish weavers to come to England to teach new techniques to improve the industry. There was also a new profession that began to appear – the mercer, a trader in cloth, with many mercers becoming families of wealth.

Tudor buildings along
Friar Street, Worcester.

Tiles were made in the Lowesmoor district of Worcester but fifteenth-century records show ornamental tiles were also made in Worcestershire. These were used in the cathedral and many other monasteries. Much later, in 1650, a thousand tiles were ordered for the repairs of the chapel in Bewdley. Old kilns were found in Malvern in 1833 and in Droitwich in 1837. In the Droitwich kilns, leftover tiles were found that matched those in the churches of Great and Little Malvern and Worcester Cathedral.

A BOY BORN TO BE KING

When Prince Arthur, the Prince of Wales and heir to the throne, was 14 he was appointed Justice of the Council of the Marches and made Tickenhill Palace in Bewdley his royal residence. On Whit Sunday in 1499 he was married there by proxy to Katherine of Aragon, with a Spaniard called De Puebla standing in for Katherine. He was aged 13 and she was 14. In 1501 the marriage took place for real and they lived at Tickenhill Palace, as well as Ludlow Castle, until 1502 when Arthur died of a 'sudden and unidentifiable illness'.

It has been said that his funeral was the most magnificent ever seen in Worcester. His father, Henry VII, wanted as much pomp and ceremony for his son as possible. Led by Thomas Howard, Earl of Surrey, the torchlit procession left Ludlow with Arthur's embalmed body conveyed through the streets under a canopy. Banners were flying and the prince's favourite horse was dressed in rich finery. The procession halted in Bewdley and Arthur lay in the chapel overnight. In the morning there was a requiem mass and a dole of two pence was handed out to the poor. Continuing to Worcester, the procession crossed the river at a ford close to Astley and entered Worcester at Foregate. Here it was met by bailiffs, priests, clerks and choir boys.

The coffin carrying the prince was then met at the cathedral by the abbots of Worcester, Gloucester, Evesham, Chester, Shrewsbury, Hailes, Tewkesbury and Bordesley and a watch, which included lords, knights, gentlemen, officers and yeomen, kept vigil overnight. Three masses were heard the following day before the body was laid in its tomb. The most senior positions in the church had already been taken by King John and St Wulfstan, so Arthur was laid in the chantry chapel by St Oswald, which became known as Arthur's Chapel. The whole occasion was so moving that many officers were visibly overcome with emotion. Strangely there were no members of the royal family present. They were afraid of the plague, which was present at the time.

A question has always been raised as to why Worcester, but it is thought that it was then the closest important church to where he died. Also, King John was buried there and, of course, his royal residence, Tickenhill Palace, was in Worcestershire.

Of course, Katherine went on marry Arthur's brother, Henry, and some years later their daughter, Mary, lived at Tickenhill Palace. At the age of 9, when her father was involved with Anne Boleyn and was divorcing her mother, Mary was sent to Tickenhill with a reduced household.

THE DISSOLUTION

As the closing of monasteries and abbeys began, desperate measures were made to try and save them. The Abbot of Evesham, Clement Lichfield, desperately tried to save his abbey. He wrote begging letters to Thomas Cromwell but to no avail. The story tells that a cellarer named Philip Hawford told Cromwell that if he was the abbot he would happily surrender the monastery. With that Lichfield was forced to resign and Hawford became abbot, for which he received a pension of £240. On Clement Lichfield's last day he took mass then quietly left, ending his days in Offenham. When his tomb in Evesham was opened many years later, a lock of his hair still remained.

The oldest part of the abbey, which is still standing, is Abbot Reginald's Gateway. It leads from the churchyard into the marketplace and dates back to the twelfth century. Also still standing is the Bell Tower, which was completed in 1539, the same year the abbey was dissolved. It was built by Clement Lichfield but with subscriptions made by the townsfolk. It was those subscriptions that helped save it from destruction.

When the monks of Great Malvern Priory surrendered, the land and buildings were plundered and all that was left was the Prior's House, the Gatehouse and Guesten Hall. Everything else was demolished. The Priory Church was rescued by the parishioners as their own church needed repair and the Prior's House was bought by John Knotsford, a sergeant in arms to Henry VIII, who was a participant in the dissolution of the priory.

Another abbey rescued by the town's people was Pershore. After seeing the nave being pulled down, together with the Lady Chapel, they paid £400 to save the east end and the tower. Two large buttresses were erected many years

Abbot Reginald's Gateway.

Evesham Bell Tower.

Malvern Priory's archway in more modern times.

Pershore Abbey now being held by buttresses.

later in 1913 as structural issues began to develop due to the damage caused during this time.

Hugh Latimer, a popular rector in Wiltshire, was a big supporter of Protestantism and this came to the notice of Henry VIII. So when he needed support with his break from Rome, and divorce from Katherine of Aragon, Latimer was made Bishop of Worcester in 1535. But Latimer was a strong character and many arguments ensued. He had been among the few reformers who raised a voice in protest against the way it had all been carried out. He did this, he said, not for the monks, but for the education that took place in these buildings. Eventually, having pleaded Pershore Abbey's case, he resigned. Having been told to pay 500 marks to the king and 200 to Cromwell, he refused. Henry wanted to have him executed but Thomas Cromwell came to his aid and Hugh continued to live in the town of Hartlebury, but was forced to sell his books, and sometimes his clothes, in order to live.

When Henry's daughter, Mary, became queen, Latimer was arrested for his protestant beliefs and together with Archbishop Cranmer was burned at the stake.

THE BIRTH OF THE LANDED GENTRY

After the dissolution, the remains of the religious houses were ransacked. A lot of demolition was actually undertaken by the local townsfolk, who used the stones to build new homes. What remained was sold to people attached to the court and many loyal followers of the king secured a good share of the monastic spoils, although some only bought them as investments. Then there were cases where estates were swapped for land that the king wanted. And when Henry VIII offered a swap you didn't argue.

All this newly acquired land brought about improvement and new craftsmanship in building and development. New houses were built on what was once church land, such as Westwood Park at Droitwich.

John Packington was a lawyer who Henry VIII admired. His family had been sheriffs of both Worcestershire and Herefordshire and the family seat was at Hampton Lovett. John had entered the Inner Temple in 1505 and after the dissolution bought thirty manors.

Westwood House wasn't built until some years later, during Elizabeth's reign, by his nephew, John, who was a courtier of Elizabeth. Having spotted him during her travels in Worcestershire, she invited him to court and promptly nicknamed him Lusty Packington because of his sporting abilities. When the house was first built, it was only used as a small banqueting house. However, when the Hampton Lovett house was burned down during the Civil War the family moved to Westwood and enlarged it.

John Packington was created a baronet in 1620 and died five years later. His grandson, John, became one of the Knights for Worcestershire in 1640 and Charles I gave him a commission to raise recruits in the county. He was taken prisoner, placed in the tower, and fined £5,000. He then joined Charles II and was again taken prisoner after the Battle of Worcester, but was so popular no one would testify against him, so was freed with a fine of £7,000. Many years later, in 1846, John Somerset Pakington (1799–1880) was created 1st Baron Hampton, after inheriting the estate from his mother's brother and taking the name Pakington.

Another who gained recognition was William Sheldon. His grandfather, John Sheldon (1380–1427), had taken up residence in Abberton following his marriage to wealthy heiress Joan Cotton. The manor was held by Pershore Abbey, so after the dissolution Henry granted it to William, from where it passed to his nephews, William and Francis. It remained in the family until 1798, when Thomas Sheldon sold it to John Hardcastle.

The Abberley estate was given to Henry's favourite page, Walter Walsh, whose family originated from Shelsey. His descendants continued to own the manor until William Walsh sold it to the Bromley family. William was both a poet and a politician, representing Worcester in the late 1600s and early 1700s.

GENTLE PERSUASION

Henry VIII had no use for the barren, marshy wastes of Bordesley Abbey but he was interested in his neighbour's estate near Hampton Court. So Lord Andrew Windsor of Stanwell, a gentleman of the royal chamber, was persuaded to leave the manor of Stanwell, an estate that had been in his family for 500 years. The family were of Viking descent, with Otho (or Othere) having settled in Middlesex before 1066. The name Other has run through the family ever since.

So on a cold, wet November afternoon Lord Windsor arrived at Bordesley. The abbey was now in ruins, so the only place he could seek shelter was a farmhouse. Accepting his lot, he began to renovate the old farmhouse and Hewell Grange became the Windsors' seat in Worcestershire for the next 400 years, although the house was rebuilt twice during that time.

As Catholics, the Windsors could have been involved in the Gunpowder Plot but the then baron had died a few months earlier and his heir was too young. Eventually, due to the line having died out and the baronetcy being continued by a cousin, the family became protestant. They fought with the king during the Civil War and Thomas Hickman Windsor was commended for bravery at Naseby by the king, and after the Restoration became Lord Lieutenant of Worcestershire. Then, as Governor and Admiral of Jamaica, he won a victory over the Spanish and was made Earl of Plymouth.

And so the landed gentry were born.

In 1569 the Heralds visiting Worcestershire reported that fifty-two families were recognised as gentlemen and had the right to bear arms.

But it was also the start of hostilities within religion and the new church. Many Catholic families refused to attend the parish church. In 1593 Worcestershire had 180 recusant families, among them the Habingtons, the Lyttletons, the Packingtons, the Talbots of Grafton, the Windsors and the Wintours.

However, a breakaway group from the new Church of England was also developing. With deep roots in preaching the Bible, the Puritans tended to exist within the lower and middle classes, religiously following the Sabbath rules that involved no sports or dancing.

THE HALL WITH HOLES

Sir John Pakington bought Harvington Hall in 1529 from the Earl of Warwick, whose family had inherited the hall from Adam de Harvington in the mid-fourteenth century. When he died in 1578 his great-nephew, Humphrey Pakington, inherited and transformed the property into a Tudor mansion.

The family were Catholics, so this led to a lot of problems for Humphrey. From 1583 he was constantly in trouble. For this reason, Harvington Hall is riddled with priest holes. Nicolas Owen, the recognised master-builder of such places, is known to have constructed four of them. When Humphrey died in 1631

Harvington Hall.

the estate passed to his daughter, Mary, the wife of Sir John Yates of Buckland in Berkshire, but his widow, Abigail, continued to live at Harvington Hall. When Mary Yates died in 1696 her granddaughter, Mary Throckmorton of Coughton Court, inherited and the family used it as an occasional place to stay up to the 1850s. But it was then left empty and became derelict until it was bought by Mrs Ellen Ryan Ferris, who handed it over to the Roman Catholic Archdiocese of Birmingham. They renovated it and opened it to the public in the 1930s.

ELIZABETH AND WORCESTERSHIRE

Queen Elizabeth I visited Worcester in the summer of 1575, riding side-saddle on a white horse with the ladies and gentlemen of her court behind her. She stopped at White Ladies Aston for refreshment and changed from her riding habit into a richly embroidered gown. Her hair, neck and fingers were strewn with jewels. Bishop Bullingham and his entourage met her at Crossway Green, close to Hartlebury Castle, where she spent the night. In preparation for her visit to the castle, new paths, known as the garden walk, had been created.

She entered Worcester the next day and stopped to admire a black pear tree, afterwards ordering that it should become Worcester's coat of arms. While in Worcester she stayed at the Old Palace and worshipped in the cathedral but she was not happy with the county. She felt there were too many recusant families here, such as those at Harvington and Hindlip.

To commemorate Elizabeth's visit to Worcestershire, a silver sixpence was specially minted.

BEWDLEY CAPS

Bewdley was well-known for making woollen caps. Made of coarse two-ply wool, seamless with a flat double brim, they were very popular with Queen Elizabeth. During her reign she proclaimed that only caps made in Bewdley were to be worn, and an Act of Parliament ensured that anyone who did not adhere to the order received a fine of 3*s* 4*d*.

A hundred years later Bewdley caps were the favourites of Dutch seamen – so much so that they were renamed the Dutch Caps of Bewdley. At that time Thomas Farloe and Walter Palmer were the names most associated with the trade. Then, towards the end of the seventeenth century, business began to decline and by the mid-1800s it had disappeared altogether.

THE BABINGTON PLOT OF 1586

Hindlip Hall was built by John Habington around 1575. On 16 August, Elizabeth I dined with the family during her visit to Worcestershire. But the Habingtons were among the many important families in Worcestershire who were Catholic and refused to convert to the Church of England. John's two sons, Thomas and Edward, were to figure in a plot to assassinate Elizabeth. Thomas had become a Catholic while studying in France and together with his brother joined the followers of Mary, Queen of Scots. Letters to Edward regarding the plot were smuggled into Hindlip Hall in beer barrel stoppers, but the conspiracy was soon discovered. Two groups of conspirators were sentenced to be hung, drawn and quartered. Edward was among the second group. However, because Thomas was a godson of Elizabeth, she spared him and he spent six years in the tower.

Returning to Hindlip, he had eleven secret chambers built there. They were so well built that, twenty years later when priests hid there in the aftermath of the Gunpowder Plot, it took many days before the wanted men were found. And then it was only because they had given themselves up through lack of air. Thomas was not arrested on that occasion but he was told he was not allowed to leave Worcestershire during his lifetime. He was then aged 47 and he died aged 87.

GLASS

It was during the Elizabethan era that Protestant refugees from Lorraine (Huguenots) introduced glass to Stourbridge. There had been earlier glassworks in Sussex but the forests that supplied the fuel were becoming exhausted, so the workers looked for an area where this was more abundant. This happened to be Worcestershire, although by the 1630s, the forests here were also disappearing and the use of wood was also eventually prohibited. Being a seafaring nation, the wood was needed for a more important industry – shipbuilding.

By the end of the sixteenth century the glass industry was well established and two families in particular have been credited with its development. Annanis Henzell and his son Joseph developed the covered glasshouse pots that produced the refined, clear sparkle characteristic of Stourbridge glass. Another refugee, John Tyzacke, had glassworks in Lye, where his glasshouse cones and kilns were part of the landscape for centuries.

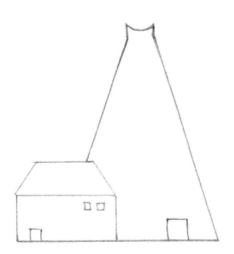

Glasshouses and their cones were a common sight
in the Stourbridge area for many years.

Although Venetian glass was considered to be superior, Stourbridge glass has always been an important commodity. By the twentieth century it was considered the finest decorative glassware in the world. In fact, before the First World War, the Kaiser was given a cut-glass ewer and basin from Stourbridge as none in Germany could be found to match the standard.

The fine clay found in Stourbridge is particularly good for the making of glass. In 1696 seventeen of the eighty-eight glass houses in England were in Stourbridge. Seven made window glass, five made bottles and the other five made flint, green or ordinary glass.

4

THE EARLY 1600S

When James I came to the throne in 1603, Worcestershire was in a strange way very much like the county of today: mainly a rural area containing market towns and villages with a certain amount of industry dotted about. Stretching from Dudley in the north, almost to Stow-on-the-Wold in the south, it lay in a shallow valley surrounded by the rivers Severn, Avon, Stour and Teme. These rivers were important to the growing industries and trade. The Severn, with its connection to the Bristol Channel and the New World, had become a busy commercial route. And with large vessels only being able to reach Bewdley, this town was growing rapidly as a transfer point. Goods arriving here were taken from the larger vessels to smaller ones, then carried further upstream or vice versa. Raw materials such as iron ore, lead and timber were carried regularly, as well as manufactured goods – food, animal skins and material. However, not all commodities had successful journeys, salt in particular. It has been recorded that from time to time large quantities of salt were lost in the Severn because of high winds and strong tides as the heavily laden vessels made their way down the river from Worcester.

The River Avon also played a part. William Sandys of Fladbury built locks at Tewkesbury, Strensham, Nafford and Evesham, which made that river navigable too.

The growth of industry was very evident by the early 1600s. The northern part of the county was already known for its metalwork but at this time was still dependent on small furnaces, which were owned by the land owners and leased to the smiths.

When iron mines, which it is thought were worked long before coal, were found in the north-east of the county the area began to develop. Dudley became the centre of this industry along with its neighbours Oldbury, Cradley, Stourbridge, Halesowen and Old Swinford.

With a plentiful source of local iron, nail making became established in Bromsgrove, Stourbridge and Dudley. Then, around the Clent Hills area, scythe making could be found. It was a skilled process from which scythe makers could become very wealthy.

The coal fields in Worcestershire were an extension of the South Staffordshire fields and stretched down the west of the county as far as Pensax. The majority of mines were found in parts of the Wyre Forest, which it is believed were being worked as early as the thirteenth century. There was also a small field near the village of Rubery, which was only worked for a short time.

Droitwich was still producing its salt and from early times 'salt ways' had spread across the county where packhorses had trod regularly. Pottery was being made in the Hanley Castle and Upton upon Severn districts, and market gardening and fruit growing was in abundance around Evesham. Tobacco was grown in the Eckington and Evesham areas, and in 1627 there were twenty-seven tobacco growers in that district. Potatoes were introduced but in those days they were not widely cultivated.

In Kidderminster the cloth trade, then known as stuff, was beginning to thrive, with master weavers taking control. They purchased the yarn, then employed journeymen weavers who were closely supervised at every stage. In 1619 an unnamed inventory mentions 'seven carpets of Kitterminster stuff'. Another belonging to Lettice, the Countess of Leicester, lists four 'carpets of Kidderminster stuff'. Of course, in those days a carpet was not something you walked on; they were used as wall hangings or drapes laid across furniture.

Other towns in Worcestershire were involved in the cloth and weaving industries but Kidderminster produced a coarser kind of wool. This was due to the type of pasture ground around the town on which the sheep grazed. Mixed with linen, this wool produced a heavier type of cloth that was ideal for carpets.

FIDDLER FOLEY STARTS A DYNASTY

Much of the growth of the nail industry was due to one man and his cunning plan. Richard Foley was born in Dudley in 1580, the son of a nail maker. He became an expert nail maker but he also played the violin and made a second income playing in local inns.

In those days the cheapest nails could be bought in Sweden so, disguised as a fiddler, he travelled there on two occasions and learned their methods; in particular the way they slit the rods of iron from the flat sheets, which cut the cost of production. However, his first slitting mill was not in Worcestershire but in Kinver, Staffordshire, but when he died in 1657 he had leases on five furnaces, nine forges and many ironworks around Worcestershire. During the Civil War he supplied cannon, pike heads, nails and other iron ordnance. He lived on the High Street in Stourbridge and was buried at St Mary's in Stourbridge.

His second son, Thomas, was born in 1616 and took over the business from his father. With the huge profits he made during the 1650s and '60s he was able to buy the Witley estate and built Witley Court in the late 1660s. He was MP for Worcestershire in 1659, and for Bewdley in 1660 and 1673. He also founded the Blue Coat School (the Old Swinford Hospital) in Stourbridge, which provided food, clothes, education and apprenticeships for sixty poor boys.

In 1712, his grandson, Thomas, was created 1st Baron Foley.

THE SON OF A LORD

Dud Dudley was born in 1598, the illegitimate son of Edward Sutton, the 5th Lord Dudley. But he wasn't hidden away. In fact, Edward took more care over the upbringing of the eleven children by his mistress, Elizabeth Tomlinson, than he did of the five children by his wife, Theodosia. Dud attended Oxford University, then, in 1618, took over the Pensnett iron forges and furnaces of his father. It was here that he first started substituting coal for charcoal in the smelting of iron.

Up to this time iron ore had been smelted using charcoal, but the supplies of wood to produce charcoal were depleting so Dud started experimenting with the use of coke. In 1621 he obtained a patent for his idea and it was very soon proving successful. His works at Hasco Bridge began producing a record amount of 7 tons of pig iron per week.

Dud was a royalist and served in the Civil War under first Prince Maurice and then Lord Astley, but after the siege of Worcester he was captured by Andrew Yarranton and condemned to death. He managed to escape the Gatehouse prison in Westminster and fled to Bristol, eventually returning to Worcester. After the restoration he published the book *Metallum Martis*, which describes his way of working in the smelting industry.

He lived on Friar Street in Worcester and when he died in 1684 he was buried at St Helen's in Worcester.

GUNPOWDER, TREASON AND PLOT IN WORCESTERSHIRE

The main conspirator of the plot to blow up Parliament was Robert Catesby, who was from Northampton, but he had cousins in Worcestershire – Robert and Thomas Wyntour of Huddington Court. The brothers recruited many of the other plotters from Worcestershire, all wealthy gentlemen from good stock, and one day thirteen would-be conspirators met in Huddington Court. It was here the plan was hatched to blow up Parliament.

It was decided that Thomas Wyntour (often spelt Wintour) would go to Flanders to enlist the help of Guy Fawkes, who was experienced with explosives. With the day getting closer, the tunnel dug and the gunpowder stored in the vaults under the House of Lords, Robert Wyntour and Robert Catesby met

Huddington Court.

at Huddington Court to finalise their plans. After lighting the fuse, Fawkes was to escape by boat to Flanders. Meanwhile, Sir Edward Digby would arrange a hunting party on Dunsmoor Heath, near Rugby, where the Catholic gentry from across the Midlands could hear of the success, or failure, of the plot. Robert Wyntour was to collect arms, ammunition and horses at Huddington, and other places, then a relay of fast horses would be situated along the roads from London to Dunchurch in order for the Princess Elizabeth, staying at Coombe Abbey near Coventry, to be proclaimed Catholic Regent.

There have been many suggestions as to how the plot was discovered. One was through an anonymous letter received by William Parker, Lord Mounteagle, which he thought had been sent by a member of his family for his own safety. Rumour has it that it was from his sister, Mrs Mary Abington of Hindlip Hall. Some have said he wrote the letter himself as he was trying to gain favour with the king. But wherever the letter had come from, he took it to officials at Whitehall and Guy Fawkes was found with his matches and gunpowder. It was also noticeable that, although no other letters came to light, other prominent Catholic members were absent from Parliament on that day.

It has also been suggested that the government was already aware of the plot and was waiting to catch the conspirators in the act, rather than arrest them with no real evidence. After all, how easy would it have been to keep all those elaborate plans a secret?

Most of the conspirators were assembled at Huddington when the news of failure was received. Thirty men now prepared themselves for death as they knew their days would be numbered. And although they knew there was probably no escape, an attempt of escape was made. After attending a mass in the hall's chapel, they decided a journey to Wales was the best option.

They rode through Hanbury to Hewell Grange. Here they obtained, or perhaps stole, arms and gunpowder before continuing to Clent, Hagley and Stourbridge. The weather wasn't in their favour as it was pouring with rain, so the gunpowder became damp – how many bonfire nights since that night have been washed out by rain?

Eventually the fugitives arrived at Holbeach Hall, near Dudley, at 10 o'clock that night with their captors hot on their heels. At about 11 o'clock the Sheriff of Worcester, with an armed force of two hundred, arrived at the house. The plotters did put up a short fight, during which a few were killed, but in the end they were captured and taken back to Worcester.

Meanwhile, Robert Wyntour and Stephen Lyttleton were hiding in barns and farmhouses around the countryside. However, after two months on the run they were given away and captured. Hiding at Hagley Park, the home of Humphrey Lyttleton, they were given away by the family's under-cook. Later, in an effort to save his own skin, Humphrey gave information about the various hiding places at Hindlip Hall. Through this information Jesuit priests Edward Oldcorne, Henry Garnett,

Nicholas Owen and Ralph Ashley were found. They had been hiding for four days with just an apple between them.

However, Lyttleton did not escape justice. Together with John Wyntour and Father Oldcorne, he was hung, drawn and quartered at Red Hill in Worcester. Robert and Thomas Wyntour and Father Garnett met a similar fate in London. The lady of the house, Meriel Lyttleton, was away at the time, so she escaped arrest.

Edward Oldcorne's head and quarters were spread out around Worcester on poles. His heart and intestines were thrown into a fire. Legend has it that the fire lasted sixteen days, even though there was continuous rain. In the end the fire was smothered with soil.

The ghost of Lady Wyntour supposedly walks along the moat at Huddington, waiting for her husband to return.

A Life in Needlework

Helena Wyntour was the daughter of Robert Wyntour and was only a child when her father and uncle were executed. She devoted her life to Catholicism and her embroidery was her daily act of devotion.

Born in 1600 she lived at Badge Court, near Elmbridge, where she sheltered priests and illegally held mass. Many times in her life she would have been in danger but she never faltered. On her death in 1671 it was her request that a school be set up at Badge Court for Catholic children.

During her life she embroidered many vestments for the use of the family priests. She designed the intricate embroidery work herself, then employed others to do the sewing of the garments. When she died the vestments were split, in equal shares, between her sister-in-law, Lady Wyntour, and the Jesuits of Stoneyhurst College. Prior to her death, Father George Gray went to visit her to find out exactly what he was inheriting. Writing of his visit, he described the fine embroidery, rich colours and the numerous garments that she had spent many years producing.

These embroideries are still held by Stoneyhurst College and in 2016 they were joined by the other half of the collection for the first time since Helena's death at an exhibition in Douai Abbey.

THE MAYFLOWER PILGRIM

Edward Winslow was born in Droitwich on 18 October 1595 into a staunch Puritan family who had originated from Earl's Croome. A branch of the family had also settled in Kempsey. Following his marriage in 1594, Edward's father, also Edward, had moved to the St Peter's parish in Droitwich, where he is said to have been a man of some substance, a landowner and farmer, although it is believed he also owned a salt mine. At some time he was also the Under-Sheriff for Droitwich.

At the age of 10 Edward was sent to be educated at the King's School in Worcester Cathedral, having been given a scholarship by the Dean of Worcester. He stayed until the age of 15 and then at the age of 17 obtained an apprenticeship as a printer in London. Four years later he left to join the Separatists in Leiden, Holland, where he helped set up a printing business with the English inhabitants there, who had exiled themselves due to their beliefs. As William Brewster's assistant he published religious books and material that were illegal in England. In fact, King James was so incensed with them that he arranged the seizure of the printing press.

Edward now came into contact with a group who, to escape religious pressures, were planning to start a colony in the New World. On 16 September 1620 the *Mayflower* set sail from Plymouth with 102 pilgrims on board including Edward, his wife and his brother, Gilbert, who was then aged 20. The ship was overcrowded, with some families having to sleep on the open deck, and due to delays, they had already spent one month on board. The journey across the Atlantic then took another three months and even when they arrived it was another 131 days before the last of the passengers actually left the ship. Incredibly, only one person died during the journey but there was also one birth, a little boy who was aptly named Oceanus.

During the first winter Edward took a leading role in exploring the locality. He also established a good relationship with the natives and negotiated with them to allow the settlers to have fishing and trading posts over a large area around their settlement. He even nursed the chief back to health with chicken soup. In importance he was ranked third behind Governor John Carver and the ruling elder Brewster.

But then tragedy struck. Despite surviving the arduous journey, his wife died and Edward consoled himself with his work. Later he was to write in his journal of more deaths – 'Of a hundred persons scarce fifty remain, the living scarce able to bury their dead.' But Edward didn't remain a widower for long. After six weeks he married Susanna White, a widow who had lost her husband and been left with two small children. Theirs was the first marriage in the New World.

Edward returned to England in the autumn of 1623 to advertise the New World and attract more settlers. To do this he published a pamphlet entitled *Good News from New England*. When he returned to his newly adopted country the following year, he was chosen as assistant to the governor. He did eventually become governor and as an ambassador for the new colony he returned to England on other occasions to promote his new home and to dispel the rumours spread about its ambiance. Edward was also instrumental in setting up the harvest celebration that Americans now call Thanksgiving.

In 1655 Cromwell, who regarded him highly, employed him as a chief commissioner and sent him to the West Indies to investigate land suitable for settlement there. Edward died of a fever during the journey and was buried at sea with a twenty-gun salute.

His brother chose to settle 10 miles north of New Plymouth and named the settlement Kerswell, after the family's farm near Kempsey, and the Winslow family is said to have accrued the most descendants of the Pilgrim Fathers.

Another family also has descendants in America today and they have continued a Worcestershire profession. Francis Fincher and Alexander Beardsley were glove makers and, following persecution as Quakers, they sold up and emigrated in 1683. They were the first to buy land in Pennsylvania and Fincher, although he declined the offer, was elected as first speaker of Pennsylvania under Penn. There are still Finchers working in the glove trade in the US today.

CRIME IN DAYS GONE BY

In the 1500s and 1600s a popular form of punishment for a criminal was being whipped or placed in the pillory or stocks. In Worcester this took place in the Corn Market for both city and county prisoners. And to make sure there were plenty of people about to watch, or take part, the usual time chosen was on market day between midday and 2 p.m. Bromsgrove also used its marketplace, whereas Upton upon Severn used the bridge leading from the turnpike gate on the road to Gloucester.

5

CIVIL WAR, COMMONWEALTH AND RESTORATION

When Charles I came to the throne he wanted to rule without interference from the politicians, so he dissolved Parliament and reigned without one for eleven years. Then he raised taxes and other revenues, and like the rest of the country, parts of Worcestershire were affected. The Vale of Evesham was very profitable with its tobacco growing trade, but heavy taxes suppressed production. The Ship Money Tax levied in 1636 also affected Worcester. The Royal Forests were sold off and parts of the land were enclosed. In Worcestershire this included Feckenham Forest and Malvern Chase. The poor, who had relied on the royal forests as common land, were affected and lost their long-established, albeit informal, usage rights and had to find somewhere else to go.

Leading up to 1640 there had been massacres of Protestants in Ireland, which led to rumours of plotting Catholics. In 1641 there were riots in Bewdley and local militia were given instructions to look out for other conspiracies during the following months.

From the reign of Elizabeth I a system had been in operation for the defence of the country and organised on a county basis. Run by the lord lieutenant of a county, these militia groups were known as the Trained Bands. In January 1642 the Worcestershire band was commanded by Lord Thomas Windsor. Parliament appealed to King Charles to hand over the control of the Trained Bands to them. He refused. Parliament was not happy, so in March the Militia Ordnance came into being, ordering the muster of arms and men in their name and appointing new lord lieutenants. In retaliation, the king ordered the populous not to co-operate and so the lead-up to Civil War began.

People were confused by the different instructions issued by the king or Parliament and many towns, such as Worcester and Kidderminster, saw riots as inhabitants argued which side to support. There were different religious beliefs and local grievances, all of which added up to an atmosphere of aggression.

At the outbreak of war, Bristol and Warwickshire were in the hands of Parliament, so it was vital for the Royalists to keep Worcestershire as a stronghold. It also gave a clear route to Shrewsbury, Hereford, Wales and Ireland.

The staunch Royalists of Worcestershire included Samuel Sandys of Ombersley, the Lygons of Madresfield, the Russells of Strensham and the Middlemores of King's Norton. For Parliament there was Sir John Wilde, a local merchant, Sir Walter Devereux of Leigh Court, Sir John Ross, Nicholas Lechmere, William Lygon, the Dineley family of Charlton and Colonel John 'Tinker' Fox, an iron master who originated from Birmingham.

THE BATTLE OF POWICK

The first encounter between the Royalists and the Roundheads took place at Powick on 23 September 1642. A detachment of between 150 and 200 men had arrived in Worcester the week before led by Sir John Byron. They were carrying a convoy of treasure being taken to the king, who was in Shrewsbury. Meanwhile, 25 miles away was a 20,000-strong army led by the Earl of Essex, a Parliamentarian. Hearing of Sir John's detachment, Essex sent Colonel John Brown with a troop of between 500 and 1,000 horse and dragoons to intercept him. They camped out close to Powick Bridge awaiting Byron's men.

Coming from another direction to Powick was a cavalry under Prince Rupert, sent to assist Sir John Byron. Seeing the men coming towards them, Brown's men panicked. In the foray many were trampled to death, while others drowned in the river.

Sir John's troop was then escorted to Shrewsbury and Prince Rupert was welcomed into Worcester with the pealing of bells at St Michael's.

Sir William Russell was among Prince Rupert's troop and was later made to suffer. His manor house at Strensham was attacked and looted by Essex's troops. However, within a couple of months Worcester was securely under Royalist command, with Sir William being made its governor.

The Trumpeter Who Wouldn't Go Away

In 1643 Colonel Sandys was the acting governor of Worcester. The city defences were strong and the garrison contained 1,500 soldiers and 300 citizens who had been fully trained.

One day a trumpeter arrived at Sidbury Gate. He had been sent by General Sir William Waller, whose men, 3,000 in total, were amassed at Greenhill. The trumpeter brought a request from General Waller asking Colonel Sandys to surrender the city. But Sandys angrily told him to leave. However, the trumpeter persevered. Three times he made the request and each time he received the governor's angry outbursts of refusal. But still the trumpeter refused to go. In those days it was the rule of war that you were entitled to a civil answer. Returning a fourth time to dispel the trumpeter, Colonel Sandys brought one of his captains with him. When the trumpeter again refused to go, Sandys ordered Captain Beaumont to fire. The trumpeter fell to the ground mortally wounded.

General Waller felt the flag of truce had been violated, so he took immediate action. His gun fire bombarded the city continuously for sixteen hours. But to no avail. The Royalist guns were far superior, so he switched his attack to the Diglis end, where he eventually managed to capture William Berkeley's house. However, this was also short-lived as Sandys managed to regain it and burn the house down to stop it being used again. The Parliamentarians were then driven from St Martin's Gate back to Greenhill.

Waller then received information that Prince Maurice was positioning himself to cut off any retreat the enemy may choose to make. So the attack was called off and Waller commandeered barges to withdraw downriver.

A CUNNING FOX

In 1643 Edgbaston Hall, initially a Royalist holding, was taken by the Parliamentarians under Colonel Fox. He used it as a base to raid other Royalist garrisons around the area. One of these garrisons was in Bewdley and the 24-mile journey would take him though occupied territory. But it was an important Royalist stronghold and the Severn navigation was commanded from there so it would be quite a coup. Also, the governor of Bewdley, Sir Thomas Lyttleton, was a personal friend of the king.

A troop of Prince Rupert's army had passed Bewdley on their way to Shrewsbury, so Fox timed the raid to coincide with this, the idea being that the small group of sixty soldiers would go unnoticed. Arriving at the gatehouse on Bewdley Bridge, Fox was questioned by the sentries on duty. He immediately ordered them to open the gates to 'admit the Prince's men'. Knowing that the nearest enemy was 20 miles away, and being used to obeying such an authoritative voice, the gates were opened. Within minutes the sentries were disarmed and the Royalists rounded up with no time to warn the governor, who lived at Tickenhill Palace. He was quickly added to the prisoners and Fox rode away with his bounty. A Royalist force was sent to try to catch him but instead of going back to Edgbaston he had ridden to Coventry.

Sir Thomas, who was subsequently imprisoned in the Tower of London, came from an illustrious Worcestershire family who had lived in the county since the early fourteenth century. One of its members, John, had been knighted by Elizabeth I but his grandson John had died in the tower for taking part in the Essex Rebellion in 1601. Sir Thomas was this second John's son and had been created a baronet in 1618. Before becoming governor of Bewdley he had been made responsible for raising Royalist troops in Worcestershire. He died in 1650.

His own son, Charles, fled into exile with Charles II after the Battle of Worcester. Another son, Henry, was captured at the Battle of Worcester and spent a few months in prison. Previous to this he had been fined for having a small arsenal of guns at the family's seat in Hagley. He had argued that as the High Sheriff of Worcestershire the weapons were part of keeping law and order.

Later the family inherited the title of Viscount Cobham. Charles's son, Thomas, married Christian Temple, whose brother became Viscount Cobham. Many years later, when the 7th Viscount Cobham died, being a distant cousin, Charles George Lyttleton became the 8th Viscount Cobham.

WORKING FOR THE WAR EFFORT

Many of the iron industries in the north now converted to war work. Cottage industries began making small parts for arms, while larger foundries supplied cannon balls. One of these was Richard Foley's ironworks in Stourbridge, which began production as early as August 1642 and also produced pike heads. New industries came into being. Powder mills were built in the spring of 1643 to produce gunpowder.

Clothing for the troops was also produced in Worcestershire, including the red and blue uniforms worn by the Oxford regiment in 1643. Many county blacksmiths had the facilities to repair muskets as well as to shoe the horses passing through.

Thomas Bushell was born in Cleeve Prior in 1593 and at the age of 15 became a servant to Sir Francis Bacon. When Bacon became chancellor, Thomas followed him to court. After Bacon's death in 1626, Thomas travelled around the country and then acquired mines in Somerset. From these he provided silver for the Royal Mint and helped finance the king. After the war Cromwell confiscated his mines and Thomas returned to Cleeve Prior but on a promise of good behaviour he was given back the lease to his mines in 1652.

THOSE DIVIDED BY THE SWORD

The Wylde family were descended from Thomas Wylde, who had lived in Worcester during Henry VIII's time. He was a clothier and descended from him there were three branches of the family. By these times one son, who was considered the head of the family, was seated at the Commandery, the Royalist Civil War headquarters. Another, Sir Edmund Wylde, was seated at Kempsey and the third, at Droitwich. Chief Baron Wylde of Droitwich was a Parliamentarian, whereas his cousin at the Commandery was a strong Royalist.

Alderman John Nash of Worcester, who was a captain of horse for Parliament, and his brother, Richard, were for Parliament. But their younger brother, Thomas, who was a barrister of the Inner Temple, was very much for the king. A descendant, Dr Treadway Nash, wrote, 'The family quarrel, on political accounts, which was carried on with the greatest animosity and most earnest desire to ruin each other, together with the decline of the king's affairs and particularly the execution of this person, so affected the spirits of Mr Thomas Nash that he determined not long to survive it.'

When Worcester was occupied by the Royalists, John Nash left the city and Colonel Dud Dudley moved into his house. But when the war ended Nash returned and turned Dudley's wife out onto the street.

A branch of the Sandys family lived in Kent and has the distinction of one of its members being one of the first casualties of the war. Colonel Edwin fought for Parliament at the Battle of Powick and was seriously wounded. His wife came to Worcester to nurse him and when he died it was said she died of grief. However, the suggestion is that she caught smallpox. They are buried together in Worcester Cathedral. His brother, Richard, was also a Parliamentarian and he fell at Edge Hill in Warwickshire.

The Ombersley branch of the family were Royalists and at the siege of Worcester in 1643 Edwin's cousin, Colonel Samuel Sandys, was Governor of Worcester.

A QUIET FEW WEEKS

Tickenhill not only played host to Prince Arthur and Katherine of Aragon, it also accommodated Charles I. On 5 June 1644 Charles was in Pershore. By nightfall he was in Worcester, where he stayed seven days. On 12 June he left for Oxford and on his way stayed at Tickenhill Palace for two nights. When he left there he was chased by William Waller. Waller's army then separated, some to Bromsgrove, others to Kidderminster and Stourbridge. For a few days the Royalists and the Roundheads circled around Bewdley, Droitwich, Worcester, Pershore and Evesham but by 18 June they had gone and there was a brief respite for the county.

THE BATTLE OF WORCESTER

There were many skirmishes during the ensuing months and some towns were eventually taken over by Parliamentary forces. Eventually the strength of the Parliamentarians took hold and on 5 May 1646 King Charles surrendered. Two weeks later, Colonel Whalley and his Roundhead army were camped on the north-east of Worcester, an area of high ground where he could look down on the city. As his army began building ditches and sconces to enclose the city, raiding parties were sent out to disrupt the work but by the beginning of June, the townspeople were getting disheartened. Soldiers deserted and joined the Roundheads and servants stole their masters' horses, money and clothing, then disappeared. But those still loyal to the king held Worcester against the enemy and they continued to build their siege lines. Eventually, on 23 July 1646, with no ammunition left, very few soldiers and very little food, Henry Washington, the then governor of Worcester, surrendered.

With the execution of Charles I in January 1649, the country started to build a new life under the power of Parliament. But Charles II was waiting in the wings. Following his father's execution, he lived in exile in France but in June 1650 returned to Scotland, where he amassed an army of Scottish supporters. As Charles and his army started a long march south along the west coast, joined by a small company of sixty men led by John Talbot, Parliament sent orders to the Worcestershire militia to rally on Pitchcroft field in Worcester. On 21 August Charles's army arrived in Worcestershire on the outskirts of Kidderminster. The people of Worcester, with the siege of 1646 still in their memory, pleaded with both armies to fight elsewhere and prepared to surrender. But the militia fought on while desperately awaiting reinforcements. The reinforcements didn't arrive and the Scots army advanced into the city during the night of the 22nd. The next day, making a grand entrance, Charles II arrived, but the city became a prison as Oliver Cromwell quickly sent men to surround it.

By the end of August 1651, the Parliamentary army had increased in numbers as men had flocked to the area from all parts of the country. They totalled around 30,000, compared with the 15,000 men Charles had with him in Worcester. The highest percentage were Scots but about 2,000 had joined Charles on his journey through England.

First the Roundheads seized the river crossing at Upton upon Severn and a platoon advanced towards Powick, while another continued up the banks of the Severn. At various stages they met opposition from Royalist soldiers and the hand-to-hand combat was fierce, but they continued on.

Charles watched the action from the cathedral tower, then rode out to Powick to encourage his troops. At first their resistance was successful and they drove the enemy as far as the Pershore road. But then Cromwell arrived on the south side and forced the Royalists back into the city. On 3 September the Essex and Cheshire militia forced their way through Sidbury Gate, while Charles Fleetwood's cavalry rode across the Severn Bridge from St John's. Around 4,000 of Charles's army were killed and around 10,000 taken prisoner, many of whom were transported to the New World.

Charles slipped back to Friar Street, where he was lodging, then left by St Martin's Gate. He and his small party of local gentry were led to safety through the Catholic areas of Hartlebury and Stourbridge to Boscobel. His surviving Scottish soldiers tried to make their own means of escape the best way they could, but how many actually reached Scotland is not known. People were eager to show their support for the new Commonwealth and took their revenge on the fleeing Scots. In Kidderminster a group were ambushed in the market square. In Chaddesley Corbett another group were killed, then buried near the crossroads in Broome. A skeleton later found in Huddington had a purse containing thirty-two Scottish copper coins of Charles I issue attached to its thigh. No doubt the soldier had been wounded and was hiding. Surely his purse would have been removed if he had been killed outright.

THE PIEBALD PONY

Sir Rowland Berkeley was born in 1613, the son of William Berkeley. William was a wealthy clothier and Sheriff of Worcester in 1617. He purchased Cotheridge Court near Worcester in 1615 and the family continued to live there for 350 years.

Rowland had vowed not to get involved in the Civil War and he later wrote that he had been taken to Worcester against his will to meet with the king and then discovered a commission had been issued commanding him to join the forces of Major General Massie. Rowland had two piebald horses, which were identical, and he rode one in the Battle of Worcester. As the battle came to an end, Rowland escaped and left the exhausted pony at a farm on his route for home. Arriving home, himself exhausted, he went to bed. Within a short time Roundheads came knocking on his door. He declared he had not been fighting but they insisted he had been conspicuous by his piebald pony, so he told them to check his stables. There they found the pony, strong and healthy, and it was obvious it had not been either involved in the battle or the escape. They left and Rowland had the last laugh.

He went on to serve as MP for Worcester in 1661 and spent eighteen years in Parliament.

A Meeting with a Tailor or the Devil Himself

Prior to the Battle of Worcester, Cromwell occupied all the high ground on the east side. The high knoll, where Cromwell personally directed operations, is still known as Oliver's Knoll. It was here, three days before battle, that a disastrous assault was made on the camp. 1,500 Royalist men were picked to get into the area and, hopefully, capture the general. In order to see each other in the dark they wore white shirts over their armour. This also made them good targets for the enemy, who had actually been forewarned and were waiting for them.

William Guise was a tailor and also a strong supporter of Parliament. Having lowered himself over the city wall with a knotted rope, he made his way to Perry Wood, where he apparently met with Cromwell himself and divulged the plans for the raid. The raid left many Royalist casualties and the ground around Battenhall was covered with bodies.

When the Royalists discovered what Guise had done he was hanged from the signpost of the Golden Goose in Broad Street the next day. However, after Cromwell had won the battle, Guise's widow was given a sum of £200, to be followed by an annual payment of £200 for life.

Cromwell died seven years to the day of his victory in Worcester, so later generations changed the story. His meeting in Perry Woods was now with the Devil, where he had bargained his soul for victory and seven years of life.

A ROUNDHEAD SOLDIER'S DESCRIPTION OF WORCESTERSHIRE

A unknown soldier described Worcester as being the largest town he had seen since leaving London. He said it was very populous and rich with an impressive cathedral that contained many stately monuments. He was particularly impressed with that of King John, which was made of white marble. However, the town itself was so vile it resembled Sodom 'and is the very emblem of Gomorrah'. He called it a 'den of thieves'. In contrast, the county was pleasant and fruitful with rich countryside filled with corn, woods, pastures, hills and valleys. Every hedge and tree was stacked with fruit, especially pears, which made a pleasant drink called perry.

It's not really known when perry was first made but the city and the county have been associated with the pear since Henry V's time. At the battle of Agincourt the Worcestershire men carried banners depicting pear trees laden with fruit and during the reign of Elizabeth I the county was described as 'abounding in pears', the juice of which made a kind of wine called 'pyrry'.

Even today the Worcestershire cricket team are known as 'the pears'.

LIFE IN PURITAN WORCESTERSHIRE

The Puritans were a God-fearing society and they wanted to create a country in their own likeness. Life was strict under their rule. The Sabbath had to be spent in prayer and Bible reading.

There was no dancing or gambling. In Cropthorne a group of men appeared in court after being reported by the vicar for playing football. In 1649 four women in Worcestershire were tried and executed as witches.

Churches were to be decorated plainly, so statues were destroyed and artistry whitewashed over. Even today, medieval paintings are being found on church walls in Worcestershire when being renovated. Three wall paintings were found on the north wall of St Nicholas's in Warndon, and in 1855 wall paintings were found in Pinvin church, which dated back to the late thirteenth century. Clergy were also not allowed to keep registers of baptisms, marriages and burials, although some kept notes hidden away that were later added to the registers after the Restoration.

There But for the Grace of God Go I

This saying is supposed to have been first uttered by Richard Baxter when he saw a man being taken to gaol. For twenty-five years Baxter was the vicar of St Mary's in Kidderminster but because of his high moral ways he was often in conflict with both his congregation and the authorities. His belief was that there should be nothing to distract a congregation from the service, in particular statues and pictures or effigies, so he had them all destroyed. But when he tried to destroy a carved crucifixion an angry crowd attacked him, so he left Kidderminster and went to Coventry. He returned in 1647 under the protection of Cromwell.

Despite his past outbreaks, he was said to be a caring man. He visited the sick constantly, acting as their doctor as there was no doctor in Kidderminster at the time. Having studied medicine, he would have known what to do. And with his kindness and eloquence he persuaded the people of his parish to abandon their immoral and lawless ways. Later in life he was still preaching against the Church of England, which brought him before Judge Jeffreys. He spent eighteen months in prison.

QUAKERS

During this period a number of religious sects were formed, known as dissenters or non-conformists.

The Quakers were founded in Evesham in 1650 and were known as the Society of Friends. However, they were treated badly, often being arrested and fined heavily. Sometimes they were beaten and whipped. Their possessions would be confiscated and their books thrown on bonfires. At other times they were kept locked up – sometimes for up to fourteen weeks in dungeons without daylight and just a small hole where their food was passed through to them.

In 1655 the Quakers were holding a meeting in a house in Bengeworth. The parish incumbent preached such an angry sermon against them that some of his parishioners marched to the house and surrounded it, shouting and hurling abuse. Eventually they dispersed and the Quakers could continue their meeting.

But for all this the Quaker movement survived and many of its members were to become prominent associates of the society and to figure in the development of Worcestershire. Many of the families who developed industry during the 1700s and 1800s were Quakers.

ANOTHER NEW RELIGION

The first Baptists appeared in 1645 and the first minister was the Rev. Dr John Tombes of Bewdley. He had been practising adult baptism while preaching in London, and when he returned to his own town in 1645 he continued to preach and administer baptism by immersion. He was opposed by Richard Baxter of Kidderminster, who challenged Dr Tombes to take part in a public discussion. This took place on New Year's Day, 1649. Large crowds from many parts of the country and various universities came along and they all decided that 'Tombes got ye better of Baxter by far'. When Dr Tombes retired he moved to Coventry, where he died in 1676. One of his protégés was John Eccles, who had been baptised by Dr Tombes. When he became a preacher in 1650 he moved to Bromsgrove and remained there for forty-seven years.

Gradually other Baptists began to spread across the county. They settled in Worcester in 1651, Pershore in 1658 and Upton upon Severn in 1670.

An Act in 1672 allowed places of worship to be established for other non-conformist groups. Presbyterians were quite strongly represented in the north of Worcestershire, with Congregational and Independents more in the middle and south.

THE RESTORATION

After his restoration, Charles never visited Worcestershire. No doubt it had bad memories, but he did contribute to the restoration fund for the cathedral.

THE BISHOP'S HOME RETURNED

Hartlebury Castle was the home of the Bishops of Worcester for many years. The land was originally given by Anglo-Saxon King Burthred of Mercia in the late ninth century, but it was Bishop Godfrey Giffard who was granted the right, by Henry III, to build a fortified castle there in 1268. The first royal visitor was Edward I.

During the Civil War it was held for the king by Captain William Sandys with a guard of twenty-one men. But on 6 May 1646, after a two-day siege, it was taken by Colonel Morgan and for a while was used as a gaol for Royalist prisoners. When its upkeep became too costly, plans were made to demolish it but it was rescued by Thomas Westrowe of Mitton, who bought it for £3,133 6s 8d.

By the time Charles II returned to England the castle was in a state of disrepair and took several years to renovate before it could once more become the home of the Bishops of Worcester. The new bishop, James Fleetwood, felt there was no need for it to be fortified, so the renovation work turned it into a country mansion, although the name 'castle' was kept.

When war once more threatened the country in 1803, with a threat of invasion by France, the king planned to send the Royal Family to live there.

In 2007 Bishop Selby, the then Bishop of Worcester, retired and it was decided by the Church Commission to sell Hartlebury. A trust was set up that eventually secured the castle and it has now become a museum. Queen Elizabeth II visited the castle for lunch on Maundy Thursday in 1980, which made her the last royal visitor in a long line of visiting monarchs.

A FARMER, A CANAL BUILDER AND AN IRON FOUNDER

Improvements were made in farming that increased the amount of food available, and new techniques were introduced. One of these was made by Andrew Yarranton (1619–84). Following years of tilling and liming, the soil was becoming dry and tired. But by growing clover in certain fields he discovered that this enriched the soil with nitrogen for the crops that followed.

Andrew was very much an innovator. In 1662 he tried to make the River Salwarpe navigable at Droitwich. His plan included building six locks, five of which were built, but then he ran out of money.

He also took an interest in iron smelting. During the Civil War he noticed the large quantities of iron slag that had been left behind by the Romans. At first he made use of them without consent but eventually did apply for permission. The slag was shipped on hundreds of boats to his main furnace in Astley where the iron was extracted.

A VIEW OF WORCESTER

During the 1670s, Thomas Baskerville, a topographer from Oxfordshire, wrote of his journeys through many counties. Of Worcester he wrote:

> The way to this city is a reddish earth, and very bad for travellers in winter, so that for the benefit of horsemen in dirty weather, they have made a causeway extending some miles from the town. As touching the city of Worcester, I think 'tis bigger than Oxford, and very full of people, but the streets, excepting that running through the city to the bridge, and another thwarting the upper end of this street, are narrow, and of old decayed buildings.
>
> Here are twelve or thirteen churches, with that on the other side of the Severn to which a fair bridge, with six large arches big enough for hoys to pass under, gives passage. This river is navigable for these kind of vessels to Shrewsbury and further, and from those parts they bring down abundance of coal to serve the city and other places beneath it, and from Bristol they bring merchantable goods up stream again to serve these parts. Along the banks of the Severn here, which is well-nigh a bow-shot over, running with a nimble clear current, are large fertile meadows, but that which is most remarkable as touching ingenuity, on the shore of the town side, is a waterwork, which, having a wheel which gives motion to suckers and forcers, pumps the water so high into a leaden cistern, that it serves any part of the city. Nevertheless, that water may be more plentiful, they have horses also at work to force up the water, and here also, which I have nowwhere else seen, save in the city of Ely, they fetch water from the river upon horses in leathern bags, to sell.

THE BRIDGE OVER THE RIVER STOUR

During the 1500s James Wilmot of Hartlebury had used land he leased from the Bishop of Worcester to build a corn mill and five fulling mills for the manufacture of cloth on the northern banks of the River Stour. The Wilmots had a distinguished ancestry, having descended from Elizabeth Woodville, the Queen of Edward IV. They were also distant relatives of Lady Jane Grey. In the 1600s they converted all their mills into iron mills and placed a few planks across the Stour to use as a makeshift bridge. However, when the river rose this bridge was impassable for horsemen. They had to travel a mile out of their way to cross the river and also trespass on Wilmot's land, for which they were charged a penny.

The bishop received numerous complaints about this so he decided a better-quality bridge was needed.

In 1681 a young man called Philip Tolley was convicted of being the father of an illegitimate child. The court sentenced him to a public penance at Hartlebury Castle – he had to stand on a white sheet with a candle in his hand. Not wanting to be seen doing this, Tolley suggested that instead he would pay for the labour of building a new bridge. All the bishop had to do was provide the materials. The agreement was made and Tolley's bridge provided a crossing for almost sixty years. Unfortunately, a disagreement between the local council and the church as to whose responsibility it was to maintain the bridge meant that it eventually fell into disrepair.

QUARRELSOME SONS

In 1679 Eleanor Dineley of Charlton near Cropthorne married Edward Goodere, who was later to become the Member of Parliament for Evesham. She bore Edward three sons and it is these sons who have a story to tell. One died in a duel, for which the reason is unknown, but the other two, John and Samuel, were to become bitter rivals with dreadful consequences. They continually quarrelled over the family estate and other family matters, as well as who should be mayor of Evesham. There was an occasion when Samuel arrived at church to find his brother sitting in the mayor's pew. Samuel was so angry he sent his servants to remove his brother. As they were in church, John felt he should control his anger, so quietly left.

Later Samuel was in Bristol as captain of the warship *Ruby*. John also happened to be there, so a mutual friend invited them both to dinner. When they left, two sailors from the *Ruby* were waiting to grab John and take him back to the ship. Here they strangled him while Samuel stood guard outside. However, they didn't get away with it. All three were tried and executed.

John left behind twin sons, of which one died a lunatic. The other was classed as just eccentric. He continually advertised for a wife, even setting up his own printing press in order to print leaflets to hand out.

THE LAST COURT JESTER

Roland Bartlett of Castlemorton is thought to have been the last country gentleman to keep a fool or court jester, a role that was now dying out. Jack Havod and his tricks were still remembered many years after his death by the people of Castlemorton. Once he was helping carry peas into a barn for storing. When there was no room for the last of the crop, he calmly shovelled them out of the window into a pool of water saying, 'we've got a vent for them now'. For centuries afterwards people of Castlemorton would say, 'We've got a vent for them, as Jack Havod said.'

Royal Favours

With the reign of James II, Catholic worship became more open and a Catholic chapel was built by Foregate in 1685. Four years later, James visited Worcester as a guest of Bishop William Thomas. He requested to see the new chapel but the town council refused to go with him. Then, when William of Orange replaced James following the Declaration of Indulgence, Thomas Morris, a canon of Worcester Cathedral, refused to swear the Oath of Allegiance to William and Mary. It was probably because of this that he was never promoted. When he died he requested to be buried at the foot of some steps in the cathedral, saying, 'I have been walked over in life, I will be walked over in death.'

The Oldest Newspaper in the Country

In 1690 Stephen Byron began publishing a pamphlet that told the gentlemen of Worcestershire what was happening around the world, and in particular, London, and how trade was faring. At first, local events weren't included as it was thought these gentlemen would only want to know what was going on outside their immediate environment, of which they already knew. But after a few years local news items did begin to appear, together with local adverts. In 1748 this newspaper was sold to Harvey Berrows and became known as the *Worcester Journal*, then the edition for 11 October 1753 bore the new name, *Berrow's Worcester Journal*. It has kept that name ever since and is still in circulation today making it the longest-running, continuous publication in the country.

6

THE GEORGIAN AGE OF IMPROVEMENT

In Georgian times the industrial towns began to grow. Kidderminster extended its borders to accommodate more carpet workers. Stourport grew rapidly from a hamlet to a fashionable town after becoming the point where the canal network met the River Severn. Great Malvern grew as a spa town offering 'water cures' after Dr Wall publicised their efficiency in 1757. Hotels were built to accommodate visitors. The streets had what we now call a Georgian appearance: tall brick houses with elegant stone quoins, sills and architraves.

Malvern's Priory Church, rescued from Henry VIII's men, would have seen many visitors coming and going.

THE SPORT OF KINGS

In 1718 an event happened in Worcester that introduced a sport that is still as popular in Worcester as it was then, if not more so. It also means that Worcester Racecourse is one of the oldest in England. It was developed on old meadows on the banks of the Severn and has become known as Pitchcroft.

The first race took place on 27 June 1718. It was open to any horse and the prize was a saddle and bridle. There were three two-mile heats and the winning horse was to be sold for £7. There was also a race for men and women around Pitchcroft. The prize for the men was a pair of silver buckles and for the women a fine hat.

In 1749 the prize had gone up to 50 guineas and in 1762 there were three races over three days. In 1822 Worcester racecourse was becoming an important course and that same year the Gold Cup was introduced. The jumping course was considered to be the best in England.

Racing in Worcester became a regular event and in 1837 two events took place: flat racing in the summer and steeple chasing in the autumn. In the 1870s there were fourteen races over a two-day period and seventy-eight horses competed for a prize of £730.

From 1858 the patron was the Earl of Coventry.

THE BLACK COUNTRY

In 1712 the world's first steam engine was built in Dudley. It was used to pump the water out of one of Lord Dudley's mines. This was the beginnings of a new age that became known as the Industrial Revolution. It also led to the growth of the industrial towns of Worcestershire.

Before the early 1700s, industry had mainly been located in rural valleys where water power was used to drive the machines. But now coal and steam became the means of power, so the

majority of industry moved to where the coal mines were. The
north Worcestershire area around Dudley not only had a wealth
of coal, there was iron, limestone and fire clay too. Soon Dudley
and its neighbours were filled with mines, forges and factories,
all packed together, with numerous streets and houses built
around them.

Together with neighbouring towns in Staffordshire, this mass
of industry became known as the Black Country. The coal dust
from the mines and the fumes and smoke that spewed from furnaces and forges certainly left their mark. Small Worcestershire
hamlets around Halesowen, Stourbridge, Lye, Oldbury and
Dudley all merged together into one blackened, smokey,
scarred district.

THE RATTLE OF CHAINS

Chain making developed out of the development of the ironworks. The making of small chains only required a fire and
bellow, similar to a blacksmith, plus a hammer. However, large
heavy chains, used mainly for shipping, required large expensive machinery, so were made by only a few firms. One of these
was Noah Hingley at Netherton, which made chains for the
Admiralty. The makers of the smaller chains, like other small cottage industries, would employ the whole family in one way or
another after obtaining their iron from a master.

HARD WORK FOR LITTLE REWARD

Further south is Halesowen and Bromsgrove and it was here that
the nail-making industry thrived. It has been said that the community of nail makers were heavy-drinking, rough-mannered
men who had wives who were worn out by work and silently
endured their life. They lived in small cottages, which contained

a brick-built, one-storey nail shop in the backyard, only lit by one very small square window and only big enough to contain a hearth and bellows, a tool rack and the workers. Here the family, including the children, would work around a circular hearth for sometimes up to fourteen hours a day. Babies would swing in hammocks and toddlers would curl up by the fire. Then at the age of 7 they started work, first sharpening the iron before making the nails alongside their parents. Sometimes they had a second profession. Farmers usually had a nail shop on their farm for extra income.

Nailers never really earned a decent living. The middle men, known as foggers, were unscrupulous and often exploited the workers. It was a well-known fact that the scales the nails were weighed on were often inaccurate. But if the nailer ever argued about it he would be told to go and find another master. And if he disagreed regularly, the nailer would find himself blacklisted and out of work.

THE HAND THAT FITS THE GLOVE

No one seems to know how far back the glove-making industry in Worcester goes. Probably back to the twelve century, or possibly even further, but there was certainly an industry there by 1497 when records show the existence of a Glovers' Guild. Then in 1561 there was a company known as the 'Glovers, Pouch Makers and Pursers'.

Up to the early nineteenth century good roads just didn't exist, so travel was very difficult. However, with Bristol being an important skin and leather district at the time, skins could be brought to Worcester up the Severn. The tough skins were then turned into fine leathers by being dressed with raw eggs. Sometimes they were softened with urine.

In the first half of the nineteenth century trade was in its most prosperous period and exports increased to staggering amounts. In 1808 there were seventy masters employing 6,000 workers. By 1825 this had risen to around 120 masters with 30,000 workers.

The glove cutting took place in workshops, where the master would work at his bench with three or four journeymen or apprentices. Then the sewing would take place in numerous cottages around Worcestershire by out-workers, usually women. It was quite normal for a skilled cutter, a male of course, to employ twelve or fifteen sewers. The master then took the finished articles to the fairs and markets, as well as his regular customers.

GLOVE MAKERS WHO BECAME WEALTHY

Even though they were prominent in civic affairs as well as glove making, the Dents ran their business the same as other masters. John Dent worked in the workshop, while his brother William did the travelling.

The business started by their father John Dent in 1777 was to become known around the world and with all their wealth, John and William were able to buy a dilapidated castle. They bought Sudeley Castle in Gloucestershire from Lord River in 1837. It had been ruined by Cromwell and renovations had been started by Lord River but all the Dents' wealth meant they could complete the work. They died within a year of each other and their estates passed to a nephew, John Coucher Dent.

THE GLOVER'S NEEDLE

St Andrew's Church was built in 1751 but now only the spire remains. Its steeple was long and thin and came to a sharp point at the top. Therefore, as a tribute to the glove industry, it became known as the glover's needle.

In 1801 a barber shaved several customers on the top of it and a local china painter decorated a cup while sitting up there. And

Glover's Needle.

when repairs were needed in 1870 a kite was used to manoeuvre the ropes for the builders' ascent.

The church became redundant in the 1940s when the slum area around it was demolished and the congregation was drastically reduced. Therefore in 1947 it was decided to demolish the church and replace it with a garden. However, the spire still remains.

PORCELAIN FIT FOR ROYALTY

By the 1750s chinaware was becoming very popular, with imports being brought in from Europe. In 1751 Dr John Wall and William Davies, an apothecary in Broad Street, Worcester, started experimenting with the manufacture of porcelain. They took out a lease on Warmstry House in Worcester and turned it into a small factory. There were pressing and modelling departments on the first floor and a warehouse on the second. There was also a painting room and kilns in the gardens. Wall was a clever chemist, and an accomplished artist, so with his scientific skills he was able to produce some of the most beautiful porcelain in Europe. Within ten years Wall and Davies were employing 200 workers.

Dr Wall died in 1776 and in 1783 the business was bought by Thomas Flight for his two sons, John and Joseph, for £3,000. While visiting Worcester in 1788, George III and his family visited the premises. After thoroughly inspecting the works, the king gave it a Royal Warrant.

Meanwhile, another factory had grown in another part of Worcester. Robert Chamberlain had been one of Dr Wall's first apprentices and after learning the trade had set up on his own. He too had become very successful and in 1840 the two companies amalgamated. Twelve years later Richard William Binns and William Henry Kerr took charge of the company and, due to the royal warrant given by George III, named it the Royal Worcester Porcelain Company.

Robert Chamberlain's brother-in-law, Thomas Grainger, had left the company in 1801 and established a third factory in Lowesmoor. This company spanned 100 years and three generations – Thomas, his sons George and Henry, and his grandson Frank. In 1902 the Royal Worcester company also acquired the Grainger factory.

A cup and saucer made by Royal Worcester in more modern times, probably in the 1960s.

The Carpet Industry

The carpet industry as we know it today started around the mid-1700s when John Pearsall began toying with the idea of making floor coverings. The idea didn't catch on straight away and it was fifteen years before the flat-weave carpet became popular. In the meantime, other weavers were also always looking for new ideas and in 1749 John Broom went to Belgium to find the secret of the new looped-pile carpet they were making. He found a weaver willing to divulge the secret and brought him back to Kidderminster. At first they hid in an upstairs room and by candlelight developed a new type of loom, but it wasn't long before other carpet weavers also began producing the new Kidderminster carpet.

John Broom joined forces with John Pearsall in 1749 and they leased land at Mount Skipet to build a factory. From here the firm Pearsall and Broom became the forerunners in the new industry. Investing in a second building, these two factories became the first carpet factories of notable size and by 1758 their buildings contained thirty-two looms.

Transporting the rolls of carpet was not easy in those early days, with only pack horses and carts available. Then in 1772 the Staffordshire and Worcestershire canal was cut through Kidderminster, and with its link with the River Severn at Lower Mitton, carpets could now be transported much more easily. The carpet industry took off and Kidderminster became the capital of the carpet-making world.

When patterned carpets were introduced and became popular, many new companies were formed and more factories appeared. And with an influx of workers arriving, new houses were built that saw the town grow.

By the late 1700s smaller factories were closing and larger ones, some containing sixty to 140 looms, were taking over. The boom continued into the early nineteenth century and between 1811 and 1831 the population almost doubled from about 8,000 in 1811 to nearly 15,000 in 1831.

Because of competition from the north, carpet manufacturers reduced the price of carpets and therefore reduced wages. This resulted in the workers taking strike action between March and August 1828. Eventually they were given a higher wage. Later in the 1850s, new steam-powered looms resulted in unemployment. This time 2,000 workers rioted, marching and throwing stones. They were eventually quelled by the Dragoon Guards.

Carpet factories were unhealthy and dangerous places to work. They were lit by candles that stood far too close to the wool for safety and only had small windows, so the smell from the dyes lingered. The carpet industry also employed young children. The child would work with a carpet weaver for many hours, sometimes late into the night if an item needed finishing. In general a working day would start at six in the morning and continue until eight in the evening, very often over a period of six days a week. However, officials checking the factories in the 1830s said the children appeared healthy, well-fed and well-clothed.

A Shrewd Clothier

In 1817 Princess Charlotte died in childbirth together with her baby. The country would be going into mourning.

George Talbot of Mill Street, Kidderminster, made a black cloth known as bombazine and it was well-known, even as far away as London. Two companies heard the news almost as it happened, so rushed to Kidderminster to buy George's stock. When they were knocking frantically on his door in the early hours of the morning, he guessed something big had happened and refused to sell anything until opening hours. This gave him time to investigate. By morning he was well aware that black cloth for mourning clothes would be needed by the masses. Needless to say, by the time he opened for business that morning the price of his cloth had risen and he made a lot of profit that day.

Through the Eye of the Needle

Needle making first came to Redditch in the twelfth century when the Cistercian monks built their abbey in the marshland at

Bordesley. The waters and the flow of the nearby River Arrow seemed perfect for the process of needle making and, encouraged by the monks, people who were setting up home outside the abbey walls were encouraged to make needles, and so the cottage industry began.

Needle wire was cut from flat sheets of iron, the ends rounded by hammering, then rubbed down using a cloth soaked with wet sand. The wire was then cut to the desired length, pointed at one end and eyed at the other. The eyes were made by flattening the end of the wire, then a small chisel was used to split it in two. The tips were then closed and welded together. The pointing was achieved with a small file and the needle was now cleaned and polished. This process was known as scouring.

By the early 1700s certain aspects of the needle-making industry were moving out of the cottages and into purpose-built mills. Scouring mills would operate continuously day and night when the water was flowing freely. But come the winter, the water might freeze and then in the summer, there could be a drought. Scourers worked twelve-hour shifts and could produce about 4 million needles in a week of very high quality.

Needle pointing machines were introduced in the late 1700s, but working them was dangerous. The dust given off by the sandstone grinder proved fatal for many workers. Working in semi-darkness, so they could see the points forming by the light of the sparks, the clouds of dust around them were invisible. Pointers were paid well but often died by the time they were 30.

Redditch became the centre of the needle-making industry and other places found it hard to compete. During the 1800s the area saw an influx of workers arriving from other parts of the country to settle in the town.

BUSINESS BOOMS, FACTORIES TAKE OVER

Symon Millward set up his needle business in 1730. When he died in 1770 his son, Henry, took over and the business became known as Henry Millward & Sons. By the end of the eighteenth century it was the largest needle factory in the district. 100 years later it was the largest in the country.

Other factories sprang up over this area of Worcestershire but the cottage industry didn't fold. Many mills employed outworkers and in 1824 it was estimated a family could produce 500 needles a week. Their cottages were recognisable by the windows, which were wide in proportion to height, therefore producing plenty of light as needle making was fiddly work.

Needle making also led to the making of a similar product and often workers would be involved in both trades. Polycarp Allcock set up his business with his son Samuel in 1803 and by 1880, Samuel Allcock & Co. were the largest and oldest manufacturer of fish hooks in the world. In 1960 they amalgamated with others under the control of an American, Henry Shakespeare. In the 1980s the company's turnover was in excess of £4 million.

With the decline in the industry in the early twentieth century some companies amalgamated to become Entaco (English Needle and Fishing Tackle Co. Ltd).

SALT ...

Salt had been an important commodity since Roman times. Many Roman roads were known as saltways as they had been purposely built to transport it. In Anglo-Saxon times a network of salt tracks had spread among the woods of Worcestershire, all coming from Droitwich, and taking the name Droitwich to all parts of the kingdom.

By the 1700s these tracks had become practically impossible to use due to all the traffic. With the wear and tear, coupled with bad weather, they were often impassable for nine months of the year. In 1713 an Act was passed (the first of the Turnpike Trust Acts in Worcestershire) for the repair and upkeep of the road between Droitwich and Worcester. In 1767 James Brindley was asked to make a survey for a possible canal between Droitwich and the River Severn. It opened on 12 March 1771. Six miles long, it was constructed as a barge canal, not a narrowboat canal, so was wide enough for the larger Severn vessels to continue their journey right up to the wharves of Droitwich.

The brine in Droitwich was originally found in springs but later from a strip of land between Dodderhill, Friar Street and High Street. At one time there were thirty-two recorded wells in this area and between the seventeenth and nineteenth centuries the brine overflowed to the surface from as deep as 80ft. When extraction began to take place in nearby Stoke Prior in 1825, the brine ceased to overflow.

Sir Richard Lane, who was at times the mayor of Worcester, heard that the salt pits of Cheshire were being sunk deeper than those in Droitwich, so, in 1725, he bored through the bottom of a pit to experiment. Strong brine gushed out with so much force that two men working in the pit were pushed to the surface and killed.

Fifty years later Joseph Priddey reported that he had sunk several pits to a depth of about 35ft. There was then a thick layer of talc of about 150ft and below that a stream of brine, then a hard rocky layer of salt. With this discovery the salt industry in Droitwich thrived. More pits were discovered in Stoke Prior in 1828, and by 1875 more salt was being produced here than in Droitwich. However, combined, the two areas produced 170,000 tons of salt a week.

... AND VINEGAR

Since 1781 Hickin Bold had owned a small vinegar works in the centre of Stourport. Needing finances in order to expand, he joined forces with Charles Swann of Tenbury and so in 1798 Swann & Company was formed. They built a brewery at Cheapside, on land between the River Severn and the River Stour, which produced malt vinegar using malt, barley, yeast, sugar and water. They then went on to experiment with other ingredients and other sauces.

For nearly 100 years the company continued to supply the country's vinegar, then in 1879, just as it had merged with J. Thompson & Co. of Birmingham, a fire ravaged through the brewery. With the large vats being made of wood, their walls bulged and the entire premises needed to be rebuilt. The Birmingham Vinegar Brewery Company bought the site and rebuilding took place in 1882.

Between 1879 and 1882 experiments had been made with pickles and sauces. One of these was Holbrook's Sauce, named after a salesman who had apparently sold more than anyone else. By 1900 this sauce was so popular that the Birmingham Vinegar Brewery Company changed its name to Holbrooks Ltd.

THE BISHOP AND THE LIBRARIAN

Richard Hurd was born in Penkridge in 1720 and earned a BA at Cambridge in 1739, then an MA in 1742. He was ordained as a priest in 1744 and became the Bishop of Worcester in 1781.

In 1782 he began to build a library, which became known as the Hurd Library. There is no other library like it today, it being an original book collection, sitting on the original shelves, which were erected in 1782. Every book you can think of, on every possible subject – history, science, theology, geography and more – can be found here. Many of the books were already old when Richard bought them. The room is long with ornate pillars and, apart from a set of windows, contains wall-to-wall books.

Housed in the Bishop of Worcester's residence, Hartlebury Castle, it is still there today.

NOT WELCOMED AT FIRST

It was said that Methodist minister John Wesley's worst experiences in the country were in the north of Worcestershire and south Staffordshire. The colliers and ironworkers here were described as having become almost subhuman due to the grind of the Industrial Revolution. People described the area as being full of squalor, violence and depravity.

Wesley's first visit was in 1749 and was not a success. He wrote of the blaspheming and throwing of whatever could be found while he preached in the marketplace in Dudley. In the end he had to seek shelter at a nearby house. His meetings were timed not to clash with church services but nevertheless he still met with hostility from church people and it became a regular occurrence for Methodist preachers to be attacked either with stones, dirt or dogs. Sometimes they even received a ducking in the village pond. And because the magistrates were church people they were not even able to get any justice. But gradually the people, who had been described as heathens, began to build chapels and when Wesley visited Dudley in 1788 he received a better reaction, afterwards writing that the den of lions the town had been had now calmed down.

In 1781, one of the earliest and most important Methodist circuits was established in Stourport, although it was six years before Wesley visited the town. On 25 March 1787 he preached at the back of a house in New Street. At the time some people were still suspicious of those who did not attend Church of England services and he was attacked by an unruly mob. Undeterred, he was back in Stourport a year later, on 21 March, to view the building of a new Methodist chapel. That October the chapel was registered for worship and two years later Wesley visited again in order to preach in this chapel.

During the building of the chapel, Stourport was chosen to be the head of the Worcestershire Methodist Circuit. This was considered a great honour. It was a large circuit covering 24 miles and also contained larger towns like Kidderminster. There was a team of ministers who all lived together in a house in Lichfield Street. They would travel miles around the circuit, preaching at various places, in all sorts of weather, rain and snow. One story tells of John Mantle who had to walk 11 miles to Frith Common through the snow. When he arrived he found his congregation hadn't expected him so hadn't opened the church. He then had to trudge the 11 miles back. Another, John Saunders, went to preach at Kidderminster on a very dark evening. Coming back, he walked along the canal path and fell into the water. It is said he complained, saying, 'Just think of it! Three times have I crossed the Atlantic, and then to be nearly drowned in a dirty puddle like this.'

The Baldwin family of Stourport were strong supporters of Methodism. In the 1800s Thomas Baldwin was a choirmaster at the chapel. He insured his life so that when he died, all the debts of the Methodist Chapel would be paid. The whole town came out to mourn at his funeral in 1880.

GIRL POWER OF THE NINETEENTH CENTURY

Following England's involvement in several wars during the eighteenth century the English and the French navies blockaded each other's ports. For many years this caused no problem as England had sufficient grain each year to feed its population. But then there was a bout of bad harvests that meant the price of bread rose dramatically. This resulted in a national uprising in 1800, later referred to as the bread riots.

Worcestershire didn't escape and one place in particular made the news. Women rallied from Redditch and its neighbouring villages and marched to Hewell Grange to complain to the Earl of Plymouth. They made as much noise as they possibly could, banging kettles with spoons and saucepans with ladles. The earl summoned other landowners and respectable townspeople and swore them in as parish constables, but they proved useless. On seeing the masses of angry women coming towards them they ran in the opposite direction, barricading themselves in a nearby public house. Some arrests were eventually made, with those women detained promising to behave themselves in the future.

BEFORE MOTORWAYS

Travel before the eighteenth century was not always very easy, or comfortable, but this was the age of improvement. By the 1700s the turnpike system was developing whereby old roads were being maintained and new turnpike roads being built. The first in Worcestershire was the Bromsgrove turnpike in 1726, which eventually reached Worcester. Then there was the Hagley turnpike in 1753, followed by the Dudley turnpike in 1760.

However, although the discomfort and the dangers were reduced, the journey might not always be straightforward. It may sometimes come to a sudden stop if the coachman spotted a friend, and it was not unknown for him to chat for five minutes or so before continuing the journey. Stopping at a certain inn for a pint of ale was always a good excuse for further delay.

But there were some stops that lived in memory for many years, as one traveller told:

At Alveley, half-way between Kidderminster and Bridgnorth. There in front of the Squirrel Inn, on a solid stone hose-block, six feet square, the like of which I never saw elsewhere, flanked with steps for the accommodation of passengers both on the road and inside, the provident care of Mrs Hobbs, the landlady, spread daily a snow-white cloth. Thereon appeared a crusty loaf, a cheese, and a dish of sandwiches, each one of which would have cut up into four, flanked by a portentous jug replete with mighty ale; while Mrs Hobbs, glorious in parti-coloured garments, smilingly bade guests eat and dine, which they did and were thankful.

In 1717 an unknown writer wrote in the Berrow's Worcester Journal:

Mr Foley of Prestwood came riding out of the Talbot archway. He was a fine-looking gentleman on a black horse; his hat was gold-laced, and his white curled wig hung down to the shoulders of his blue coat. He wore great riding-boots and a fine long sword; his cloak, his saddle-cloth and pistol-holders were all stitched with gold. Behind him, three servants in livery rode, armed with swords and blunderbusses, for Mr Foley was a gentleman and was riding to London.

The Toll Keeper Who Stopped a King

On 5 August 1788 King George III and Queen Charlotte visited Hartlebury. Robert Sleath was toll keeper at the Barban Gate toll house on the Droitwich and Ombersley road to Worcester. George III's journey to visit Richard Hurd took him through this toll gate and an equerry was sent ahead to advise the toll keeper. Now Robert Sleath was an honest but blunt man, and during an earlier conversation with a group of friends had said that the king, if travelling in a social way, should still be liable to pay the toll. He further said that if the king ever came to Barban Gate, Robert would not let him pass if a toll was not paid. So when the equerry arrived at the gate, Robert had no qualms in asking for the toll and he was not deterred by the threats made by the equerry. In desperation, as the royal carriage neared the gate, the equerry promised that the money would be paid by the person following the king. So Robert opened the gate and the distinguished cavalcade passed through. But there was no one at the end of the procession to pay Robert.

The following day George III returned and the same equerry was sent ahead to request the toll gate be opened. This time Robert insisted that the gate would not be opened until the toll for both days was paid. As the king's carriage came to a halt and George III began enquiring as to what was happening, the equerry had no choice but to pay.

A NEW WAY TO TRAVEL

The River Severn was becoming very busy, so following the success of the Bridgwater canal in Lancashire, named after its innovator, the Duke of Bridgewater, local investors put forward a request to build a canal between the Severn and South Staffordshire.

Francis Egerton, the 3rd Duke of Bridgwater, lived like a hermit and was obsessed by the idea of combining the four main rivers of England by a network of canals. Of course, the Severn was included, with the others being the Trent, the Thames and the Mersey. He had previously employed James Brindley to construct the first canal to take coal from his mines in Worsley to Manchester, so he asked him to survey two other canals. One joined the Trent and the Mersey and the other was the Staffordshire–Worcestershire canal, which opened in 1768.

The authorities of Bewdley refused the cutting to enter the Severn in their town, so new plans were drawn up. To everyone's surprise, Brindley chose an area of sandy waste where the Stour met the Severn at Lower Mitton. That sandy waste became Stourport-on-Severn and quickly grew into the busiest inland port in the Midlands. By 1783 it had iron and brass foundries, carpet manufacturers, tanneries (one of which claimed to be the largest outside London), and a vinegar works, as well as warehouses on its wharfs and a town centre of houses, shops and public houses.

Where possible, canals followed the contours of the land. However, in places, mountains of earth had to be piled up to carry them across valleys. Pairs of navvies would shift the earth using a wheelbarrow and pulley system. One had an empty wheelbarrow, the other a full one travelling up and down the increasing slope.

In 1791 work began on a canal linking Worcester to Birmingham. It was a difficult one to build as it went through some of the steepest hills of the county, in particular a steep gradient near Tardebigge. Initially John Woodhouse designed a boat-lifting machine. The idea was that the boat went into a lock, then both the boat and the lock were lifted to join a stretch of water on a different level and so on. But the concern was that the lifts might be prone to breaking down with so many moveable parts involved, so further plans evolved. The result was the longest flight of locks in England for narrow boats. There are fifty-eight in total and thirty of them are at Tardebigge, where they rise 217ft. At the bottom of this flight is a tunnel 580 yards long. Further along, north of Alvechurch, the longest tunnel in England was built at 2,726 yards. It runs under the Wast Hills.

The canal took nearly twenty-five years to build and was eventually opened in 1815.

The Boat People of Worcestershire

There were three types of vessels on both the river and the canal: narrowboats, barges and trows. Trows were useful in shallow water as they were flat-bottomed boats, but they could be up to 100ft long with masts as high as 80ft. If the river became too shallow, even for them, bow'olliers (boat haulers) would drag the boat through the mud and slush.

Pig iron, iron rods and other ironware, coal and salt, wool and carpets, glass and leather goods were carried from all over Worcestershire by boat. Whole families would live and work on their boats. Babies were born on them and people died on them. Boat people were often buried far from their home towns.

It was a hard life on the boats and barges, which very often had only one room (cabin) or perhaps two. They were cramped conditions for a large family but in 1877 an Act limited the number of people allowed to live on board. Then an 1884 Act made it compulsory for boat children to have some form of schooling. Public houses along the canals would provide a school room for these children. One pub in particular is known to have done this, the Black Swan in Stourport.

The discovery of steam power bought a new type of boat but these were used as passenger ferries. By the mid-1850s passengers were carried between Worcester, Holt Fleet, Upton upon Severn, Stourport and Tewkesbury. More for convenience than pleasure, they were the bus service of their day. Eventually they did become pleasure boats and in the 1900s these highly polished and varnished steamers took day trippers up and down the river.

Towpaths were introduced between 1799 and 1812, and horses now replaced the bow'olliers. Horses were hired out to the boat owners and undertook short journeys before being replaced. However, this was not accepted at first. There were many riots, and gates were nailed across the paths to prevent the horses passing. On one occasion eighty men were committed for trial.

BANISHED NUNS

In 1792 Worcestershire became a home for refugees of the French Revolution. A group of English nuns of the Order of the Poor Clares were banished from their convent in Dunkirk and returned to England. Dejected and homeless, they were given shelter in Churchill by Robert Berkeley, who lent them the Manor Farm. Their story has been saved for posterity on a gravestone near the churchyard gate: 'Here repose bodies of the English Nuns of the Order of the Poor Clares, who, when banished from Dunkirk by the fury of the French Revolution, about 1792, found refuge at Churchill.'

A GEORGIAN PERSONALITY

Perhaps the most well-known personality of the Georgian era is the Prince of Wales. He had numerous followers who wished to bask in his glory, but not all were successful. Bishop Robert Carr of Worcester was one of these.

Before coming to Worcester, Carr had been Bishop of Brighton and it was here he met the Prince of Wales. This friendship brought about numerous debts. When he died in 1841 the bailiffs arrived to claim his furniture and belongings. Under the laws at the time a body was also considered part of an estate and a saleable item. So on the day of his funeral the bailiffs claimed the body. It was only thanks to some of his friends pledging their own properties that the funeral was allowed to continue.

GEORGIAN EXTRAVAGANCE

Throughout the 1600s the ironworks of the Foley family in north Worcestershire had supplied the navy with its iron, but in the last years of the eighteenth century the family's fortunes went into decline.

Thomas Foley, who at one time was MP for Droitwich, followed a life of gambling, extravagance and debauchery. His lifestyle was so bad he figured in a Regency caricature as Lord Balloon. Such were his gambling habits that, apart from the title, his father disinherited him and left the estate to his grandson. Unfortunately he turned out to be as bad as his father, with a wife who was also just as bad. She was said to be the most extravagant woman in England at that time. With five maids attending

Witley Court.

her, she never wore a pair of gloves for a second time, or a ribbon twice, and she always had four ponies saddled and bridled ready should she suddenly decide to go out. Sliding panels were constructed at the family home of Witley in order for servants to take cover if Lady Foley was seen walking their way. She didn't want to come face-to-face with any of her servants.

The Prince of Wales, later George IV, often visited Witley. The billiard room was situated next to the chapel and quite frequently, during a quiet moment in a Sunday service, the sounds of the balls, bad language and oaths could be heard.

When the 3rd Baron died in 1833, in order to pay off his debts, his son was forced to sell Witley Court. It sold for £899,000, which was said to be the largest sum on record for a property in England in those days.

A LORD GETS HIS OWN BACK

Viscount Valentia, later Earl of Mountnorris, spent thousands of pounds converting Arley Hall, once the home of the Lyttleton family, into a replica medieval castle.

He was certainly a colourful character and had many varied interests. He collected shells and was said to have the largest in the country. His interest in nature and exploration took him on many journeys, as far away as the then Abyssinia. But his main passion was for fireworks and he spent hundreds of pounds each year on achieving the best displays. He even employed a member of staff as a powder monkey whose only job was to prepare set pieces for these displays. Much to the annoyance of his neighbours, he would stage these displays at any time without warning, sometimes in the middle of the night. When he increased the size of the lawns on his estate, he used a neighbouring patch of consecrated ground, and the removed gravestones were then used as shelves in his wine cellars.

But his 'piece de resistance' was achieved when he wanted to buy a house in Upper Arley. The house was owned by

Sam Wilcox, the landlord of the village inn, who refused to sell it. So Valentia decided to build a tower close to it. When it was finished this mini castle, with a tall castellated tower, completely ruined Wilcox's view.

THE LARGE COUNTRY HOUSE

The eighteenth century was also the age of the mansion house. These splendid country houses with large estates of parkland and farm began springing up all over Worcestershire. They were either maintained through the profits of an industry that had taken off, or from the rent of tenants. The owners of these palaces were from many backgrounds. They were politicians, colonels or industrialists who enjoyed the life of 'the lord of the manor'.

Thanks to this new lifestyle, people like Capability Brown and Humphrey Repton found lots of employment in the grounds of these magnificent mansions.

THE WAYWARD WIFE

Thomas Vernon was born in Hanbury in 1655 and came from a distinguished line that went back to Richard, Lord Vernon of Normandy. His great-grandfather, the Rev. Richard Vernon, came to Hanbury Church in 1580 and his son, Edward, bought the manor of Hanbury.

Thomas became a barrister who practised in the Court of Chancery for forty years, and was also the Member of Parliament for Worcester between 1715 and 1721. He amassed a large fortune with which he built Hanbury Hall.

When Thomas died he left no children, so the estate passed to his cousin, Bowater Vernon, and then to Bowater's son, Thomas. When he died in 1771 the heir to his estate was his daughter, Emma, who was still only a teenager, but once she came of age

Hanbury Hall.

her mother decided it was necessary to find her a husband. A good match was certainly found because on 23 May 1776 Emma married Henry Cecil, nephew and heir of the 9th Earl of Essex. The wedding took place at St George's, Hanover Square, London.

As was normal in those days, Henry took over the running of Hanbury Hall and immediately started making changes, altering the interior and removing various outbuildings to other parts of the estate.

Perhaps Emma was bored and felt neglected because when a new curate arrived in Hanbury, in 1783, she quickly took an interest in him. William Sneyd became a frequent visitor to the hall, both dining and sleeping there, and within a year Emma and William had started an affair. The affair continued for six years. Whether her husband was aware of it and took notice, or was totally oblivious, is not known, but on 12 June 1789 Emma told Henry she wanted to go into Birmingham to meet friends. Henry accompanied her there, leaving her at the Hen and Chickens Hotel. When he went back to fetch her she had left. He then discovered that William Sneyd had also been at the hotel and they had left together.

Emma and William played the part of a married couple, going by the name of Mr and Mrs Benson and renting various homes down in the West Country. Meanwhile, having accrued debts through an extravagant lifestyle and making the alterations to the hall, Henry Cecil was forced to sell all the contents of Hanbury Hall and move away. He filed for a divorce from his errant wife and on finding she was divorced, Emma married Sneyd in Marylebone on 13 October 1791. William's health was not good so Emma decided they should move abroad. He died in August 1793 and Emma returned to England, staying with friends in Surrey. Here she met John Phillips, whom she married on 28 January 1795. They took up residence at Winterdyne near Bewdley.

Henry Cecil died on 1 May 1804, so through his wife, John now inherited Hanbury Hall and the couple moved back. With the hall having been left empty, a lot of renovations needed to be done, which the couple undertook fervently. But their happiness was short-lived. Emma died on 21 March 1818 aged 63.

She was buried, wrapped in the sheet that had covered William Sneyd's body, not in the family vaults but on the northern borders of the church. Was this her choice? Some say it was. Others say it was the decision of the vicar, who had known of the disgrace she had brought the family.

However, it is said that her ghost still haunts the corridors of Hanbury Hall. A figure dressed in black has been seen taking the route she would have taken to visit her lover.

AN OLD ANTIQUARIAN

Any history book about Worcestershire should dedicate a few lines to Dr Treadway Russell Nash, a clergyman who became the renowned historian and antiquarian of Worcestershire.

Born in Clerkenleap, Kempsey, on 24 June 1725, he was the son of Richard Nash, a turkey merchant, and Mary Berkeley. Clerkenleap had originally belonged to the Winslows and after they had set sail on the *Mayflower* the estate had been bought by

John Nash in 1650. John Nash was a Member of Parliament in the 1640s and after his death the estate passed to his nephew, Richard, who was the grandfather of Treadway. John Nash and his brother, Richard, were Parliamentarians during the Civil War but a half-brother, Thomas, was a Royalist and, as already mentioned, Dr Nash wrote in his works about their quarrels and animosity.

The Nash family was well-established in Worcestershire and there are several monuments to them in St Peter's Church, Droitwich, as they owned numerous acres of land there, as well as nearby Ombersley and Claines.

Richard Nash had also exchanged land in Shrawley and Martley with the Foley family for the estate of Impney in Droitwich. Then, in 1720, he had bought Abbot's Wood near Pershore.

Treadway was educated at King's School in Worcester before moving to Worcester College in Oxford. He took a BA degree in 1744, aged 19, then an MA between 1746 and 1747. Following his studies he went on a grand tour of Europe with his brother, Richard. They were away for two years. First they spent six weeks

St Peter's Manor, home of the Nash family.

in Paris, then moved to the Loire Valley before travelling around the rest of France and Italy. Returning in the summer of 1751, he became the vicar of Eynsham in Oxfordshire. He also took a post as a tutor for Worcester College in Oxford and during this time taught a member of the Winnington family of Stanford Court, near Malvern, who were barons and Members of Parliament for Worcestershire. It is not known which member of the family he taught, but it was obviously something he broadcast at the time.

Nash married Margaret Martin in 1758 and moved to Bevere Manor in Claines, later building Bevere House. An unfortunate incident happened in 1759 when he was having furniture and goods moved from London. A fire in the wagon carrying his belongings, caused by a faulty bottle of *'aqua-fortis'* (now known as nitric acid), meant the loss of a large collection of books and pictures. In May 1761 he became the incumbent at St Peter's in Droitwich and bought Barnes Hall, an old priory estate.

Treadway's interest in history was immense and he had always had the notion that a collection of historic information about Worcestershire should be established. In June 1774 he asked people to donate material for this collection and sent sixty-six forms out to each vicar around the county. Unfortunately not many took up the idea, as he was to comment later:

Above twenty years ago, coming into possession of a considerable real estate in this my native county, I determined, as far as was consistent with a proper attention to my own affairs, to serve my countrymen and neighbours by every means in my power. Thus, I became a mere provincial man, confining my ambition within the ancient province of Wicca, commonly known by the name of Worcestershire. I had often times wished that someone would write the history and antiquities of the county. I proposed the undertaking to several persons, offering them all the assistance in my power. I invited the Society of Antiquaries to choose a proper person, promising to open a subscription with three or four hundred pounds. Failing in success in all my applications, I offered my own shoulders, however unequal to the burthen, reflecting that though very little had been published, yet this work was in some degree made easy, because materials had been collecting for near 200 years.

In 1781 Treadway's *Collections for the History of Worcestershire* was published and is still a vital tool for local historians today.

During his time at St Peter's he had a plate installed celebrating the lives of his parents, brother and sister. At the time his own name was also inscribed but the date of death was left blank until 1811, when he died at his home in Bevere and was buried in the family vaults at St Peter's.

A BOXING MATCH

Boxing was a vicious sport and bare-knuckle fights took place wherever there was a suitable space and for however long it took for one of the fighters to collapse or give in. One such fight took place at Pitchcroft in 1824 between two fighters called Spring and Langan. The fight had already lasted many hours in front of a crowd of around 40,000 people, who became quite riotous. An enormous crush ensued that resulted in many casualties being rushed to the nearby hospital. However, when they arrived, it was discovered that nearly all the available doctors were out watching the fight.

UNRULY INHABITANTS

The Wyre Forest was one of King John's favourite hunting grounds and deer continued to roam for hundreds of years afterwards. Here local tanners foraged for bark for their burners and wagonloads would be carried back to their workshops. The wood colliers, also known as charcoal burners, who provided the fuel for the iron foundries, lived like gypsies in these woods. And they were not always law-abiding. Known as the Far Foresters, they lived like bandits, poaching and stealing sheep.

Usually they were left alone, but in 1833, the parish officials of Bewdley decided the Far Foresters should pay their rates to the church and so three overseers walked the long distance between the town and the forest. They then went from hut to hut handing out demand notices. But they didn't collect anything. The men were nowhere to be seen and all they received from the women in the huts were jeers, foul language and contempt. They were told in no uncertain terms to bring their coffins with them the next time as they wouldn't be leaving the forest alive.

SITTING ON THE BORDERS

Elizabeth Barrett Browning is not a Worcestershire lady. She was born in County Durham in 1806 and moved to Hope End in Colwall, Herefordshire, when she was 3. But being practically on the border with Worcestershire, her walks often took her over the Malvern Hills. In 1832 she wrote in her diary:

> We walked thro' the rocky passage and sate down upon the Worcestershire side of the hills. Such a sight, such a sea of land, the sunshine throwing its light and the clouds their shadows upon it. I looked on each side of the elevated place where I sate. Herefordshire all wood – undulating and broken – Worcestershire throwing out a grand unbroken prospect, and more than Worcestershire to the horizon. One prospect attracting the eye by picturesqueness; the other the mind, the sublimity.

7

THE VICTORIAN AGE
OF PROGRESS

The reign of Queen Victoria began with a country begging for reform, and this often caused periods of unrest due to the Chartist Movement. In the centre of all of this was one man who had been born in Worcestershire.

Thomas Attwood was born in 1783 at Hawne House, Halesowen, and lived there through his childhood. His father, Matthias, was a wealthy iron manufacturer who owned several large estates, including the Leasowes, which was the home of his daughter. Hawne House was famous for its cherry orchards and, until the early 1800s, was

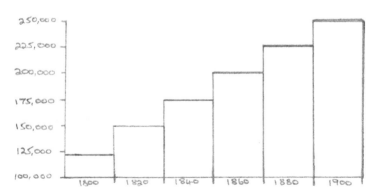

The population of Worcestershire rose steadily during the 1800s, from 120,000 at the start of the decade to 250,000 at the end.

the venue for an annual wake celebrating the ripening of the fruit.

Thomas attended Wolverhampton Grammar School, then worked at a bank. He became interested in politics and believed Parliament needed more people with business experience. In 1815 he put forward an idea to use paper money instead of gold, saying it would be better for the economy. Even though 40,000 people signed the petition, the government was not convinced.

Fifteen years later, on 25 January 1830, around 10,000 people attended a meeting of the newly formed Birmingham Political Party at which Attwood was the main speaker. Then for two years he campaigned for parliamentary reform. Following the Reform Act of 1832, he and Joshua Scholefield were elected as Birmingham's first MPs.

In the late 1830s he worked hard in the fight for the working man to have the right to vote, although he didn't approve of some of the aggressive actions taken by some Chartists. In June 1839 he presented a signed petition of 1,280,000 signatures, but it was rejected. Frustrated by the government's approach to reform, he resigned and continued his banking career. He died in Malvern in 1859.

THE CARPET INDUSTRY GROWS

The carpet industry had expanded out of Kidderminster to Lower Mitton and Stourport. Factory dye houses needed to be on the river and at Lower Mitton the River Stour split for a short distance, creating an island. This island was just the right size on which to build a factory. Robert Shirley opened his factory in around 1825 but others followed. Samuel Broom built a spinning mill close to Lower Mitton Bridge, which he named the Mitton Works. There was also Fawcett & Watson and Richard Smith & Sons. But the one most associated with the carpet industry in Stourport was Bond Worth.

William Henry Worth had opened a factory in 1831 but when his younger brother, Thomas Bond Worth, joined him, the company became known as Bond Worth. In 1853 they moved to Samuel Broom's mills in Lower Mitton, where they remained for many years.

THE FALL OF THE GLOVE

While some industries prospered during the Victorian age, others fell into decline. This was the fate of the glove industry in Worcester.

The 1824 Act allowing the import of foreign gloves came in from July 1826 and work in Worcester practically came to a standstill, with local trade being undercut by foreign imports. By 1840 business had become so bad that a deputation visited the Bishop of Worcester to ask him to assist in raising a fund to help the stricken workers. They also asked him to give Queen Adelaide a pair of Worcester-made gloves, hoping for her approval. Two years later there were proposals made by Robert Peel to reduce the duty on gloves. Worcester glovers met with Sir Thomas Wilde, telling him if this happened, many businesses would have to close. He stated the case for them in Parliament, but to no avail. In 1844 the duty on gloves was reduced.

Gloves were still made in Worcester but not to the extent they had been. Every effort was made to increase production by using new modern methods and machines but some parts still needed to be made by hand. The smaller firms, or those working singularly, ceased to trade, allowing the larger firms to continue as best they could.

After twenty years import duties were abolished in 1860, but it was too late. By 1885 there were only eleven glove manufacturers left and no cottage industry.

THE SAUCE OF WORCESTER

In 1823 two local chemists, John Wheeley Lea and William Henry Perrins, opened a chemist shop in Worcester along Broad

Street. In 1837 they began bottling a sauce that is now known the world over, Worcestershire sauce.

The recipe was a secret and, so the story goes, was brought back from India by a local man who asked them to make a jar for him. They made more than was needed but when they tasted it they didn't like it, so stored it in their cellar. Coming across it again eighteen months later, they tasted it again and realised its maturity had given it a much more pleasant taste. They made more and when they eventually started selling it, it was a great success. The well-known orange label featuring the name Lea and Perrins was introduced in the 1890s.

The familiar bottle of Worcestershire sauce.

A 21st Birthday Present Fit for a Queen

Roland Hill was born in Kidderminster in 1795. His father ran his own school, so Roland himself finished his education at the age of 12 and began teaching there. The family wasn't very well off and the thing Roland always remembered as a child was his mother dreading the postman knocking on their door, as very often she hadn't enough money to pay him. So after working as a school master, inventing a water wheel and a printing press, helping in reform and the colonisation of South Australia, Hill began to look for a way of cheapening the postal service.

The Penny Post was accepted by Parliament in 1839 and introduced on 1 May 1840. Later that month, the queen celebrated her 21st birthday.

The invention of stamps brought a new structure that is so familiar today – the postbox. Some, typical of the Victorians, were very impressive. Dr Chaffy, the local parson, built two pillar boxes in Rous Lench and Radford. Standing high on their plinths, with shallow steps leading to the box, they resemble miniature summer houses.

Victorian postbox in Rous Lench.

A Long-Serving Earl

The manor of Croome d'Abitot was bought by Thomas Coventry in 1592. He became King's Sergeant to King James, then in 1606 a Justice of the Court of Common Pleas. That same year he became Sir Thomas Coventry. The family prospered and in 1628 his son, Thomas, who was a lawyer and politician for Droitwich, became the 1st Baron Coventry of Allesborough.

The founder of this illustrious family had been John Coventry, who was born in Coventry but became a mercer in London. In 1416 he was Sheriff of London and was a close friend of Richard (Dick) Whittington.

The family continued to prosper as lawyers and recorders of the City of Worcester. But by the start of Victoria's reign they were in crisis. The then heir, Lord Deerhurst, who had become known as 'the simpleton Deerhurst', died young from consumption, which had worsened following a bad cold. Then George William, the 8th earl, got involved in long, angry and hostile political disputes over the Corn Laws. He died in 1843 from what was said to be 'an unsound mind'. This idea of 'an unsound mind' possibly showed itself in 1840. He was at a dinner in the Guildhall, Worcester, and was given an anonymous letter that accused him of being a disgrace to his title and an outcast from society.

His grandson, George, inherited the title of 9th earl when he was only 5 years old and went on to live a long life playing the role of the Victorian country gentleman. He acted as the head of the Tory Party for the county and as the local magistrate. Then, when the Worcestershire County Council was formed, he served as a county member for forty years. He died in 1930 aged 92, having been earl for eighty-eight years.

A MAN OF MEDICINE

Charles Hastings was not a Worcestershire man by birth but was adopted by the county due to his career starting in Stourport. He was born in a village close to Ludlow in 1794, where his father was rector of Bitterley Church. They were a family of fifteen but nine of his siblings died as children. Tragedy also struck when his father fell from his horse when Charles was aged 12. Taken home in a dazed state, he never recovered and remained a 'lunatic' until his death aged 101.

Hastings became an apprentice to Richard Jukes and Kenrick Watson, whose chemist shop was at 23–24 Bridge Street, Stourport. After two years he was persuaded by his employers to take a post at Worcester Infirmary as a house surgeon. Described as a tall handsome young man with a dynamic personality, he was also a born leader and his workaholic attitude led to his commitment to making improvements. A colleague once wrote that he would enter a meeting 'with the velocity of a steam engine'.

One of the first doctors to use a microscope, Hastings was also an adversary of the stethoscope and founder of many medical journals. But he never forgot his mentors, Richard Jukes and Kendrick Watson. Their contributions were frequently included in his journals, which were the forerunners of the *British Medical Journal*.

Hastings fully believed the country's health and welfare was the responsibility of the state and through his persistence, the General Board of Health was established in 1848. The previous year Hastings had become Sir Charles Hastings. He died in 1866.

RAILWAYS

The canals had been a boon in their time, with many factories and workshops appearing along their banks, but in the Victorian age a new form of transport was on the horizon. As good as the canals were, they had their difficulties. The Worcestershire–Birmingham canal, for instance, had fifty-eight locks to negotiate and was quite narrow. So, as welcome as it was in its heyday, it was not necessarily good for the new age of commercialism. Then it lost its largest transport company, Pickfords, to the new form of transport.

Suggestions for a railway link between Birmingham and the Severn Estuary were taking place as early as 1824. But it wasn't until 25 September 1835 that a committee of investors met at the Star hotel in Worcester. In April 1836 the idea received royal assent and the Birmingham and Gloucester Railway became the first train to run through the county. The first part of the line was opened on 24 June 1840. This line ran between Cheltenham and Finstall, near Bromsgrove. The whole line was opened on 17 December 1840.

While the B&GR line was being constructed, the railway commissioners were already planning where to construct other lines. A route was needed to connect Worcester with the Welsh coast, so a trunk line was built in 1840 to join the Chester and Holyhead route. But not all planned routes went ahead. In 1842 a branch line was suggested to connect Evesham with the B&GR line at Eckington, but due to opposition by local landowners it was abandoned.

The Birmingham and Gloucester Railway didn't run through Worcester. All the promoters were interested in was a direct line between the industries of the north and the port of Bristol. A branch line to Worcester was going to cost £60,000 and Worcester City was told it would have to foot the bill. It refused, so the nearest station was at Spetchley and a horse omnibus took passengers from Worcester to the station. It held fifteen people and the journey took around forty minutes.

By 1844, with trade declining in the glove-making, porcelain and metal goods industries, a group of tradesmen decided to build a line hoping this would improve trade. The line would go through Worcester from Oxford then on to Stourbridge, Dudley and Wolverhampton. A company known as the Oxford, Worcester & Wolverhampton Railway (OW&WR) was chosen to build the line, but it was to become known as the Old Worse and Worse due to its unsatisfactory plans. It wanted to use a broad gauge of 7ft, whereas other lines, approved by a royal commissioner, were using a narrower gauge of 4ft 8½in.

The old railway bridge across Foregate Street, Worcester.

Therefore the Worcester line would not connect to other lines. Five years later, with Worcester still waiting for a train service, the work was handed over to the Great Western Railway. The Oxford to Wolverhampton line opened in 1853.

Worcester had got its railway station, but it wasn't just used for passengers. At the Butts a siding was built to enable racehorses to be brought to the course. Theatre companies used the train when coming to perform at the Theatre Royal. The train would arrive with all the scenes, props and masses of costumes.

In 1861 a line to Hereford connected the area to the coal mines of Wales. Cheap Welsh coal could now be brought easily into the county. Then in 1863 construction began on a line that extended the Birmingham to Redditch line out to Evesham. This proved to be an advantage to certain companies as instead of their goods having to negotiate the Lickey incline, they could go via Redditch and still be connected to the Worcester–Oxford line.

By the 1880s the country was covered with a network of railways and business was booming thanks to the speed of trains compared with the canal barges. Heavy iron and metal goods from Dudley, quarry stone from the Lickeys, salt from Droitwich, fruit from Evesham and many more items could now be transported all over the country with ease.

Towns such as Malvern had an influx of visitors as the tourist industry began to emerge. Lady Foley, who owned most of the land in Malvern, had campaigned hard to bring the railway to her town, even though it meant building a 1,567-yard-long tunnel through extremely hard rock. Unfortunately this tunnel proved too small when trains became larger, so a second tunnel had to be built in the 1920s. The old one proved useful in the Second World War though. It was used to store torpedoes.

THE RAILWAY'S FIRST CASUALTIES

The first casualties of a railway accident in Worcestershire were Thomas Scaife and Joseph Rutherford.

On 10 November 1840 an engine boiler exploded in Bromsgrove Station and two engineers with the Birmingham and Gloucester Railway got caught in the blast. Scaife died instantly, Rutherford the next day, and they were buried side-by-side in Bromsgrove Churchyard. The inscription reads: 'My engine now is cold and no water does my boiler fill. My coke affords its flame no more, my days of usefulness are o'er.'

However, the first actual rail death recorded in England was of William Huskisson of Birtsmorton Court. As MP for Liverpool he was attending the opening of the Liverpool and Manchester Railway on 15 September 1830. He was travelling on the same train as the Duke of Wellington. When it stopped at Parkside railway station near Warrington he alighted to go and greet the Duke but at the same time Stephenson's *Rocket* was travelling on the adjacent line. It hit Huskisson and crushed his leg. He died a few hours later.

SPA TOWNS

Worcestershire may be inland, far away from the sea, but it did become a holiday resort. Great Malvern, Tenbury Wells and Droitwich all welcomed visitors to 'take the waters'; however, Malvern was the most popular. This was mainly due to its hills, which people could enjoy walking around as well as relaxing in its waters.

When two doctors, James Wilson and James Manby Gully, arrived in Malvern in 1842 they turned the small hillside village into a bustling attraction. Using the local water, they built hydropathic establishments where visitors paid large fees for treatment. A treatment also included diet and exercise. Visitors came in their thousands to partake in ice-cold baths and minimal food and to refrain from smoking and drinking. They were watched over closely by Dr Wilson. Whoever they were – peers, politicians, generals – they were all treated like boys at a boarding school. And if anyone sneaked out they were soon discovered by Dr Wilson, who rode along the hills on his thoroughbred bay mare looking for them.

One patient, Lord Lytton, felt the pangs of hunger and absconded to the town and the nearest pastry shop. Leaving the shop with a dozen tarts, he bumped into Dr Wilson. Seeing the tarts, the good doctor cried out 'poison!' and told Lord Lytton to throw them away, which the lord did without argument.

On the other hand, Dr Gully was more lenient, using a persuasive manner rather than a harsh, strict one. Probably due to this, he was more successful. Among his patients were many eminent Victorians such as Gladstone, Disraeli, Tennyson and Dickens.

In 1836 the brine baths were opened in Droitwich. They were designed for various treatments but especially rheumatism, and were operated by Mr Gabb and Dr Bainbridge. Later, in 1887, John Corbett built the St Andrew's Brine Baths, opposite the Raven Hotel, which he also enlarged. He also built the Park Hotel. This was all done with the idea of Droitwich becoming a tourist attraction.

A QUEEN IN WORCESTERSHIRE

For a short period the Dowager Queen Adelaide came to live in Worcestershire. She was the tenant at Great Witley from 1843 to 1846 and was a popular figure in the area. Unable to walk far because of her health, she regularly travelled the countryside in her carriage, with two horsemen galloping in front. The elegant four-seater carriage was an open barouche, with two large wheels at the rear, two small ones at the front and drawn by four horses. She would travel with two grooms at the rear, hidden behind a folded hood, with her coachman sitting on a seat at the left of each pair of horses. They wore royal livery and were said to be 'a sight to behold'. She spent many evenings in Worcester at the theatre and became an important member of county society.

In September 1843 her sister-in-law, Victoria, Dowager Duchess of Kent (Queen Victoria's mother), came to stay and both ladies visited Ombersley Court for dinner. They were then taken to the parish church, where they signed the flyleaf of the baptism register that was then in use. Their signatures were witnessed by Lord Lyttleton of Hagley Hall and the Rev. Talbot, vicar of Ombersley.

A Village Made by the Working Man

Feargus O'Connor, who belonged to the Men's Working Association, was appalled by the long hours workers were having to work in dreadful conditions for just a pittance. He noted in particular the nailers of Bromsgrove. However, he had an idea where workers could own their own houses. More importantly, if the working man owned his own house of sufficient value he could also vote.

In 1845 O'Connor founded a company with capital of £5,000. This had been raised by the workers themselves, 5,000 in total, by buying shares. With this he bought two acres of land for building houses. The first one built in Worcestershire was just outside Bromsgrove and was named Dodford.

Unfortunately the scheme was short-lived. In 1851, when subscribers ceased to subscribe, the money ran out.

The Lost Baronetcy

The Sutton family of Dudley originated in Staffordshire. John Sutton, as a Member of Parliament, became the first Baron Dudley. His son, Edmund, was born in Dudley but pre-deceased his father. It was therefore John's grandson Edward who inherited the title. From 1525–28, Edward was chamberlain to Princess Mary. His son, also Edward, then succeeded him in 1532 but through money problems lost the castle to his cousin, John Dudley, the Duke of Northumberland. Dudley had risen through the ranks and as regent for the young King Edward VI had received his dukedom in 1551. But later, having lost favour, he was executed and the castle was returned to the Sutton family. The fifth baron accrued many debts so his granddaughter, Frances, was married off to Sir Humble Ward, Baron Ward of Birmingham. However, in 1757 the baronetcy of Dudley fell into abeyance when Ferdinando Dudley Lea died with no male heir.

Ferdinando did, however, have two sisters, Frances and Anne. Frances married a Walter Woodcock and had two daughters, Anne and Mary. Anne married William Wilmot and they had a son, George, while Mary married a Benjamin Smart. In the 1800s George Wilmot could be found collecting taxes at the toll gate of Cooper's Bank, within sight of Dudley Castle, his ancestral home. Robert Smart, the son of Mary, was working as a grazier and butcher in Halesowen. Did they know they were descended from this ancient ancestral family?

The other sister, Anne, married a William Smith and her family fared better. Many years later her great-grandson was to make an appearance. In 1916 the abeyance was lifted in favour of Ferdinando Dudley William Lea Smith, who was a lieutenant colonel in the Worcester Regiment, and he entered the House of Lords on 9 May 1916 as the 12th Baron Dudley.

ROAD RAGE IN THE 1800S

Bishop Henry Pepys was Bishop of Worcester from 1841 to 1860 and lived at Hartlebury Castle, the seat of the Bishops of Worcester. One day he decided to go walking without his bishop's garb, just an ordinary pair of trousers and jacket. He was walking along the lane through Hartlebury Common, which at the time was the main coach route between Kidderminster and Worcester, when he heard a coach coming furiously up behind him. The driver was swearing and thrashing the horses. Stopping the coach, Pepys told the coachman to be more careful, whereupon the driver told him to mind his own business and threatened to teach him a lesson for meddling. Leaving the bishop behind, the coachman was then informed by one of the passengers to whom he had just spoken. He was horrified, stopped the coach and rushed after the bishop to apologise. However, Pepys thought he was chasing him so he began to run. When the bishop arrived back at the castle, the driver was close behind him so he slammed the door as quickly as he could. With this the driver began ringing on the bell. A footman answered and the coachman explained what had happened and that he wanted to apologise. With this the bishop came to the door and reprimanded him again over his impatience.

Bishop Pepys was also famous for baptising the daughter of a Zulu warrior in Worcester Cathedral. The father and his wife, from the Amaponda people, were exhibits in a fair at the time.

THE STRANGE MARRIAGE

The Witley Court estate was bought by Lord William Humble Ward, Baron of Birmingham, in 1838. He was only 18 when he succeeded to that title, which included an income of £100,000. He owned 200 mines in the Black Country as well as numerous ironworks. Despite this wealth, he was always in debt. He was obsessed with jewellery and thought nothing of spending money on expensive items. On one occasion he spent £60,000 at the Vienna Exhibition. At Christmas his tree was decorated with strings of jewels, and all the gifts he gave his guests came from Cartier's of Bond Street. It was said that when the famous Dudley jewels were exhibited he could not be persuaded to leave and had to be taken into custody by a police sergeant.

In 1851 he married the beautiful and rich Constance de Burgh. Her heart was elsewhere but her parents insisted on the marriage. It was a union that turned out not only to be strange but tragic too. Ward worshipped his wife but had strange ideas about how to treat her. He kept her like a possession, as he would one of his precious stones, which he also lavished on her. Her friend, the Countess of Cardigan, said she was often 'literally ablaze with diamonds'.

Ward would often expect his wife to sit for hours on a black satin-covered couch, completely naked apart from a string of pearls, while he sat and admired her. Frightened and disgusted by this behaviour, she appealed to her parents but they told her it was all part of married life.

Eventually she took a lover, Lord Dupplin, who was spotted by Ward leaving the house one day. Accusing her of adultery, he threw her out of the house and told her she was no longer a wife of his. Although she managed to get to her parents' house, they wouldn't let her in. From there she went to her singing teacher's house and stayed the night there. The next day she travelled to Ostend and lived on the Continent for the next few months, where she discovered she was pregnant. She died in childbirth and her body was returned home for burial, upon which her husband shocked his friends by forcing her mouth open to show them her rotten teeth.

Ward became the Earl of Dudley by a new creation in 1860 and in 1865 married again when he was 48. His bride, Georgina, was only 17.

Despite his odd attitude to marriage, Ward has been noted for some good things, one being the restoration of the cathedral. And he was also patron of the local yeomanry, the Queen's Own Worcestershire Hussars, who benefited greatly from his involvement. He paid for all the saddles and the officers' uniforms. His social standing and influence also enabled them to keep Pitchcroft as a place for their military exercises. One person influence he later kept company with was the Prince of Wales who, by the 1890s, had chosen Witley Court as his favourite place and often visited, expecting big shoots and extravagant parties.

THE ARTIST

Thomas Botts was born in Kidderminster in 1829, the son of a spade handle manufacturer. He started work in his father's factory but, discovering he had an artistic talent, took an apprenticeship with William Haden Richardson at his glassworks in Wordsley. Here he learned the techniques for acid etching on flute glass. But he wanted to do more serious art, so he went to Birmingham and found work as a portrait painter and japanner. In 1852 Botts moved to Worcester and was taken on by Kerr and Binn's Porcelain Works, where he became one of their main artists. He created many pieces that eventually ended on the tables of many members of the aristocracy.

Towards the end of 1869 Botts noticed that his work wasn't as perfect as it had been, and within months he was unable to work. He died on 31 December 1870 of what is now thought to have been lead poisoning contracted through the paints he had used all his working life.

THE KING OF SALT

John Corbett was born on 12 June 1817 in Brierley Hill, the son of Joseph and Hannah. Joseph was a boatman working the canal between Birmingham and Stourport, and the family lived in Delph, Brierley Hill. Certainly humble beginnings for someone who was destined to become a Worcestershire businessman and gentleman of great regard.

At the age of 10 Corbett left school and started working on the canal with his father. He had obviously had some kind of education in those few years he spent at school, as he became an avid reader of engineering books. It was his ambition to become an engineer and eventually, in 1840, his dream came true; he became an apprentice at the Leys Ironworks in Stourbridge. After serving his apprenticeship, his father took him on as a partner. But the canals were now in competition with the railways and the business was eventually sold to the Grand Junction Canal Company. Perhaps this was a blessing in disguise because, now out of work, Corbett found himself employment in 1849 at the Stoke Prior Salt Works. For the next three years he learned all about the salt industry; first as an engine driver, then an out-rider and finally a cashier.

By 1852 the salt industry was going through a bad patch and the Salt Prior Company, being only a small concern, was struggling. On the brink of closing, Corbett took over the lease and, having intently studied the reasons for past failures within the company, was determined to make a success of it. Using his engineering experience he developed new salt-refining techniques and, taking out loans and mortgages other industrialists would have never dreamed of, he proved successful. By the 1860s he owned the lease of the works and was busy expanding and improving. In the 1870s he was employing 500 workers and by 1876 was probably the largest salt manufacturer in England. On average his 30-acre site produced 200,000 tons of salt a year. Ten years later it was producing 300,000 tons. He had four brine pits, fifty canal boats, 400 railway vans and 5,600 workers.

Corbett was a good employer and looked after his workers, building them homes, a school and a church. They were given opportunities to enjoy life with organised social clubs. In 1881 he built Salters Hall specifically for their enjoyment. He also provided his workers with better working conditions. Men, women and children were all crammed together, day and night, practically naked because of the heat in the salt sheds and John could see this was not acceptable. He encouraged the women and children to stay at home and gave the men higher salaries to make it easier for families to work this way. Later he allowed women to work in the packing sheds.

Corbett also dabbled in politics. Although his first try at becoming an MP in 1868 failed, he was elected in 1874 as the Liberal candidate for Droitwich. He was re-elected three times in succession, then retired at the 1892 General Election.

By the 1880s there was a lot of competition with the salt works from Cheshire. One salt maker, Herman Falk from Winsford, Cheshire, set up the Salt Union, which aimed to bring together all the salt works in the country. Many joined his scheme, including John Corbett. Now in his 70s, John wanted to retire, but his sons weren't interested in taking over the firm so he made the decision to sell the Stoke Prior works to the Salt Union. He died in 1901 and his precious salt works closed in 1912.

A Castle Fit for a Princess

John Corbett met his future wife, Anna O'Meara, in Paris in 1855. He was 39 and she was only 24. She was of Irish decent but as her father was a British diplomat in Paris she had grown up in France. John and Anna married on 7 April 1856. After the marriage they came back to live at Rigby Hall in Bromsgrove. The couple had five children: Mary Eliza in 1858, Anna Camille,

The Château Impney, which eventually became a hotel.

1859, Anna Matilda, 1861, Walter John, 1867, and Roger John in 1867. There was one other daughter, Clare, born in 1874, but John always denied that she was his daughter.

It was not a happy marriage and Anna was homesick, missing her Parisian lifestyle. So John built her a French château in the style of Louis XIII on his Impney estate. Built between 1873 and 1875, it cost £250,000 and 3,000 workmen were involved in its construction. When completed it stood majestically on a hill in a 155-acre site, surrounded by gardens, parkland and water features. He also made a play of the French word for raven – *corbeau* – being similar to his own and used a raven as his coat of arms.

However, the marriage didn't last and eventually Anna moved to North Wales. When John died he left the estate to his brother, Thomas. The only mention of Anna was a line in his will that said: 'Whereas my wife is already provided for, I do not intend to make any further provision for her in my will.'

HYMNS

Astley is only a small village but it is famous for two things: Prime Minister Stanley Baldwin lived there in the last years of his life and the religious poet and hymn writer Frances Ridley Havergal was born there in 1836. A devout Christian, Frances's father was rector at Astley. She was a very clever child and learned to read aged 3. She studied Latin, Greek and Hebrew as well as several modern languages. A gifted pianist, she began writing verse when she was 7.

Frances wrote seventy-one hymns, with her father helping with some of the music. In 1846 he became the incumbent of St Nicholas's in Worcester, so the family moved there for fifteen years before he moved to Staffordshire. Frances became a governess and lived in both Bewdley and Stourport.

She died in Swansea in 1878, having moved there the year before. Her body was brought back to Astley for burial.

LEFT WORCESTERSHIRE FOR FAME AND FORTUNE

Ellen Price was born in Worcester in 1814, where her father was a glove-maker. In 1836 she married Henry Wood, so becoming Mrs Henry Wood, the name for which she is best known. He was a banker and they moved to the south of France for twenty years before returning to live in London.

She started writing as a child, including work on the lives of Lady Jane Grey and Catherine de Medici, but she did not keep any of these earlier compositions. At the age of 13 it was noticed she had curvature of the spine. Her growth was affected and her height never exceeded 5ft. She also had to spend time in reclining chairs and couches.

After the success of *East Lynne*, her most famous novel, which was published in 1861, she wrote another thirty novels and over 100 short stories.

She died in 1887 and is buried in Highgate Cemetery, but she was not forgotten as a Worcestershire heroine and a statue of her was unveiled in Worcester Cathedral in 1916.

Alfred Edward Houseman was born in Bromsgrove in 1859, the eldest of seven children. His father was a solicitor and the family lived at Perry Hall. His grandfather was the vicar of St Michael's in nearby Catshill and when his mother died when he was 12 and his father became bankrupt, the family moved to his grandfather's house, the Clock House, in Fockbury. Alfred now had a 2-mile walk to the Dame School he attended in Bromsgrove. This resulted in him becoming a regular, solitary walker, with his solitary thoughts eventually becoming verse. Despite not being a regular walker in Shropshire, his book *The Shropshire Lad* has become one of the best-selling books of poetry.

Houseman left Worcestershire when he went to St John's College Oxford and then went to work as an accountant in London before taking up the post of Professor of Latin at University College. In 1911 he moved to Cambridge as Kennedy Professor of Latin and died there in 1936. As a tribute to his book of verse he is buried in Ludlow, Shropshire.

His poem 'In Summertime on Bredon' relates the scenery around Worcestershire: 'Here of a Sunday morning, my love and I would lie and see the coloured counties and hear the larks so high, about us in the sky.'

Matilda Alice Victoria Powles was born on Commandery Road, Worcester, in 1864, the second of thirteen children. Her father was a comedy actor and occasional theatre manager.

During the 1850s and through to the 1930s the most popular form of entertainment was the music hall, and one of the favourite types of acts that appeared in Victorian music hall was the male impersonator. So that was how the 6-year-old Matilda started her career. At the age of 11 she changed her name to Vesta Tilley and became a big star, touring both Europe and America. She also appeared in the first Royal Variety performance.

In 1914 she was persuaded to encourage young men to enlist in the armed forces so, dressed in a khaki uniform, her shows were filled with patriotic songs. Officials were on hand to sign the young men up and those who didn't enlist were handed white feathers as they left the theatre. Unfortunately as the death toll rose, resentment began to be felt for the music hall and Vesta Tilley herself. So after the war she retired and assisted her husband, William de Frece, in his political career. She died in 1952.

THE LEGEND OF THE BLACK DOG OF ARDEN

At one time Bordesley Abbey was said to have been the fifth richest monastery in England and it was all due to the sale of its wool. At one time there were 1,650 sheep grazing on the meadows around Bordesley. In 1312 Guy de Beauchamp, Earl of Warwick, hid from Edward II at Bordesley Abbey. He had upset the king by having Piers Gaveston's head chopped off. Piers had been a friend of Edward's before he became king and the barons considered him a bad influence. He was tried in a rudimentary court by the barons, found guilty and executed. Piers had nicknamed Guy 'the black dog of Arden' because of his swarthy appearance and his tactics on the battlefields – slicing heads off with one sweep of his sword. A friend of Piers eventually poisoned Guy in 1315 and he was buried at Bordesley Abbey.

James Woodward was born in 1833 and spent his childhood in Birmingham. An accomplished writer and artist, he moved to Redditch as a young man, where he worked as a teacher. He quickly became interested in the ruins of Bordesley Abbey, so much so that he organised excavations at the old site.

During those excavations a large stone coffin was unearthed containing human bones. As it was not in the cloisters, or the cemetery, James determined that it could not be the remains of a monk. So, for some reason, he decided it was the remains of Guy de Beauchamp.

As he felt the find was so important, he stayed all night guarding the coffin. In the early hours he heard a noise and saw a large black dog with blazing eyes leap out of the darkness. He picked up a crowbar to hit it but it simply disappeared. Telling the story,

Ruins of Bordesley Abbey left behind by Henry VIII's men. Redditch villagers used its stonework to build their own chapel in the 1700s.

James said it was obviously Guy de Beauchamp angry that his coffin had been disturbed.

The stone coffin still lies among the excavations but what happened to the bones?

HAVE YOU SENT TO TELL MY MOTHER?

On 17 March 1869 a pit belonging to the Earl of Dudley known as the Nine Locks Pit flooded and thirteen men were trapped. The rescuers were cut off by a subterranean lake, so large that an engine pumping 540 gallons of water a minute was of no use. Four hours after the disaster the lights went out and the trapped men were plunged into darkness. As the lights were failing, they each wrote notes on tobacco paper that were placed in a tobacco tin. The only food they had was what they had taken down the pit with them for their lunches. When that was eaten they resorted to chewing on their shoelaces.

The eldest man, who was over 50, had got separated from the others. They could hear him calling for his wife, Louisa, until he eventually died. The youngest was a boy aged 14. They measured the passage of time by noting when the thumps made by the forge hammer above them stopped, denoting a change of shift. Eventually after six days the rescuers reached them. Having been cramped up for so long the miners could hardly move and the permanent darkness had made them temporarily blind, but at least they were alive. As each man was brought out of the shaft the crowd gave a welcoming cheer. As the boy was brought out his first words were, 'Have you sent to tell my mother?'

WORCESTER EXHIBITION 1882

The Great Exhibition of 1851 in London had been such a success that many others in the country had taken place, and someone thought it would be a good idea to have one in Worcester. The buildings that had housed the Worcester Engine Company and the West Midlands Wagon Company were now empty, so they provided ideal premises. The exhibition opened in July 1882 and continued until October.

On the opening day the streets were lined with flags and bunting, and the church bells pealed. People lined the streets to watch the brass bands and marching soldiers. Exhibits included industrial displays from across the country, together with items of metalwork, china, needlework, furniture, books and over 600 paintings. There were also architectural drawings, including the design for the new church at Upton upon Severn.

It had cost £8,500 to organise the exhibition, which made £10,044. The profits were used to help build the Victorian Institute.

THE FRENCH ARRIVE IN WORCESTERSHIRE

Wood Norton was inherited in 1887 by Louis Philippe Robert, Duc d'Orleans, from his uncle, who was the son of King Louis Philippe of France. He had been born in Twickenham in 1869 and was actually the rightful heir to the throne of France.

However, he lived like a king in Worcestershire. The 400-acre wood and mansion house became the centre of a high-class lifestyle with its own zoo and museum. Many high society and royal guests visited regularly.

CRICKET

The Worcestershire County Cricket Club was formed in March 1865 but during the previous two decades a team had played regularly in the county and also at two of the top schools at the time, Malvern College and the Bromsgrove School.

It is possible that cricket had been played in Worcestershire since the early 1800s. There were two teams then – the City of Worcester and the Worcestershire County Club – but on 5 May 1855 the two sides merged. A meeting was held at the Star Hotel and a club entitled the Worcestershire County Club was formed with an annual subscription of half a guinea. It was also decided that lower-class workers and labourers could join for a subscription of 5s per year. They were allowed to play on three nights a week and could play with the half-guinea members on one night a week. Ground at Pitchcroft, by the racecourse, was acquired. However, the club seems to have disappeared by 1857.

Then in 1865 another meeting was held at the Star Hotel that saw the creation of the Worcestershire County Cricket Club. Lord Lyttleton was elected as president. In fact, it was just two years later that an all-Lyttleton family team played at Hagley Park against Bromsgrove School and won by ten wickets. The team comprised the 4th baron, his eight sons, and two of his brothers. The team's ages ranged from 10 to 50 years old.

The first permanent ground for the team was at Boughton. Then in 1896, Paul Henry Foley saw an area of farmland on the opposite bank to the cathedral that belonged to the cathedral. It was three fields with a hedge running through the middle of it and a hayrick. He leased the ground and the team has remained there ever since. Sitting on the banks of the Severn with its view of the cathedral, it is said to be one of the most attractive grounds in England. However, being in such close proximately to the river there is rarely a winter when the ground isn't flooded.

The Earl of Coventry also played a vital part in the development of the club. At the age of 25, he was a player described as a slow lob bowler and a hard-slashing batsman. He was also a patron and administrator until his death, aged 91, in 1930. His two sons, Henry Thomas and Charles John, also played for the county. Charles was reported killed in action at Jameson, South Africa, in 1896 and a service of commemoration was arranged at the cricket ground. Just as the service was about to start, news came through that he was alive, so a party of celebration was held instead.

8

1900 – A NEW CENTURY, A TIME OF CHANGE

By the 1840s the Severn was a busy, commercial river. Traffic had increased since it had become connected to the canal system, and with the Industrial Revolution having taken place further upstream it had perhaps become one of the greatest commercial waterways in the world. But it had been a great river for many years. It had led many people to the heart of the kingdom – the Romans, the Saxons, the Danes, the Normans and many other industrious groups of people in history. For nearly thirty years the Romans had furnaces stretching along the river, bloomery workings they were called, and fields of iron slag have been left as evidence, particularly between Broad Street and Pitchcroft in Worcester. The Danes raided and looted and the Normans transported their Caen stone up the river to renovate the cathedral. From the late 1500s the Severn became a great industrial river carrying coal and iron. Every tributary seemed to have a forge or a furnace. But the river also brought unwelcome guests too. Press gangs and smugglers frequented the quays and taverns. The Black Death used the river to spread to the county and its neighbours. The plague of 1637 was brought upriver by the Bristol trow-men.

Fishing was the livelihood of many people living by the river. They worked in groups using the Severn Long Net, a large piece of plain netting that had two men holding the front, known as the headers, and two at the back known as the muntlers. There were strict restrictions imposed on these fishermen by the local landowners but despite this they caught enough salmon, for which the Severn is famous, to sell in shops or on the street.

In the mid-eighteenth century the traffic peaked, with 100,000 tons of coal a year being moved downriver. At that time there were eighteen river coal tax collectors in the country and seven of them were stationed in Worcester, which shows the importance of both the Severn and the city. Boats of 60 tons could reach Ironbridge, those of 40 could reach Shrewsbury, and small boats could get as far as Welshpool. It was 220 miles from the Welsh mountains to the Severn Estuary and the river was busy along a high percentage of those miles carrying pig iron from the Forest of Dean and salt from Droitwich. Pottery was brought from Broseley and Coalport to be decorated in Worcester, then continued its journey downriver. Worcester's own pottery also travelled the same way. There wasn't anything that was made in Worcestershire that didn't use the river at some time.

River Severn and the Worcester skyline.

However, that was all to change at the end of the nineteenth century. The railways could reach all parts of the country and so the last vessel to dock in Worcester did so in 1900. The river now gradually became a river of amusement as small pleasure boats replaced the grimy cargo vessels.

Up until around 1905 farming had still been a major form of employment for the people of Worcestershire but by the 1930s this had been reduced to only one tenth of the workforce. Nearly half the population was employed in manufacturing, with the largest industries being metal and engineering.

ISLANDS WITHOUT A COAST

Down the years the boundaries have changed on numerous occasions, and at one time Worcestershire had more islands than any other county, that is small parishes that lay in the neighbouring counties, such as Blockley.

But in the 1900s those boundaries began to change. With the 1911 Birmingham Extensions Act, Yardley, Northfield and King's Norton were taken into the City of Birmingham, and the ragged edge along the south of Worcestershire was straightened when six parishes between Bredon and Broadway fell into the county.

In 1930 there was a change with the borders of Warwickshire and Gloucestershire. Worcestershire lost Alderminster, Shipston-on-Stour, Tidmington and Tredington to Warwickshire and Blockley, Chaceley, Cutsdean, Daylesford, Evenlode, Redmarley D'Abitot, Staunton and Teddington to Gloucestershire. However, it gained Ipsley and part of Bickmarsh from Warwickshire and Ashton under Hill, Aston Somerville, Childswickham, Cow Honeybourne, Hinton on the Green, Kemerton, Pedworth and parts of Beckford and Forthampton from Gloucestershire. Dudley also transferred to Staffordshire. In total Worcestershire lost 5,832 acres.

MUSIC TO STIR THE HEART

In 1873 William Elgar ran a music shop along the High Street in Worcester. He was also the organist at St George's Catholic Church in Worcester. Much in demand by many influential Worcester families, he also worked as a piano tuner. Meanwhile, back at his shop, his 16-year-old son was getting frustrated being stuck behind the counter, but he was learning to play the violin and was proficient enough to give lessons himself. And it wasn't long before he started composing.

Edward Elgar had been born in Broadheath on 2 June 1857 and educated at Lyttleton House School. He began making public appearances playing violin and organ aged 15. In 1879, aged 22, he was the conductor of the attendant's band at the Powick Lunatic Asylum. Then he joined the William Stockley Orchestra in Birmingham in 1882. On 13 December 1883 the orchestra performed Elgar's composition, *Serenade Mauresque.*

In 1886 Caroline Alice Roberts, the daughter of Major General Sir Henry Roberts, became a pupil of his. They married on 8 May 1889 and moved to London, where he worked as a professor of music. They returned to Worcestershire in 1891 and made their home in Malvern, where he began to earn a reputation as a composer, with *Serenade for Strings* appearing in 1892. This was followed by many other works including a choral piece, *The Light of Life*, in 1896. In 1899 his *Enigma Variations* were first performed and now Elgar became recognised as a leading composer. Perhaps his best-known work, the *Pomp and Circumstance Marches*, premiered on 19 October 1901.

He was knighted in 1904 and became the University of Birmingham's first professor of music in 1905, a position he remained in until 1908.

In the 1920s his music was not as fashionable, so when Caroline died in 1920 he more or less retired, leading a quieter life pursuing hobbies and only spending short periods composing.

However, in 1924 he was appointed Master of the King's Music and in 1926, taking advantage of new technology, began making recordings of his works.

In 1932, for his 75th birthday, the BBC organised a festival of his works. Elgar once again found the desire to start composing. Unfortunately the works were never completed. He died on 23 February 1934, leaving an unfinished third symphony, a piano concerto and an opera.

FOSTERSHIRE

In the early 1900s an era began that earned Worcestershire the name Fostershire. Seven brothers, sons of the Rev. H. Foster, who was house master of Malvern College, all played cricket for Worcestershire over a period of nearly twenty years.

The eldest of the brothers was Harry Foster. After playing at Oxford for four years and captaining Malvern for one, he led Worcestershire in their first season in the county championship. He stepped aside in 1900 for his brother, Reginald, but then took the lead again from 1901 to 1910 and again in 1913. He played his last match in August 1925 aged 51.

Reginald Erskine Foster was born in 1878. He was so good that in one season he scored two separate hundreds in one match on three occasions. He went to Australia with the MCC team and scored 287, breaking all test match records. Known to his friends as 'Tip' Foster, he died of consumption in 1914. On the day of his funeral the flags at Lord's were flown at half-mast.

Wilfred Lionel Foster was in the army, so he only played twenty-nine games over a twelve-year period. Geoffrey Norman Foster played in 1903 and Maurice Kirshaw Foster began playing, aged 19, in 1908. The following year he was captain and went on to play for Worcestershire until 1934.

THE WORKING HOLIDAY

Once a year, during August and September, the countryside of the Teme Valley would be filled with people of the Black Country enjoying the fresh air. But they weren't there on holiday; they were there to work. They had come to pick the hops. Hops had been used for beer-making since the mid-1500s and the western part of Worcestershire was ideal for growing them as the soil is particularly rich there.

The pickers would arrive at the local stations and would be taken by farm wagons to their places of work. They had come from the slums of Dudley, Smethwick and other places in that district and had looked forward to it for months. However, the conditions in their summer homes were far from perfect. They slept in tents, cowsheds or pigsties, or just out in the open by a camp fire. Some, but not all, were lucky enough to be provided with some form of bedding; some were also given a bowl of soup each night. But some were just left to fend for themselves and some were even locked in at night because they were considered untrustworthy. A clergyman writing about them in the *Berrow's Worcester Journal* described them as barbaric. He wrote that although they were heard singing hymns, in the same breath they would swear and relate obscene things. And they thought nothing of going into the church or chapel to steal the benches or chairs for firewood. He also described how one mother had bathed her baby in a frying pan. But, despite the clergyman's perspective, hop picking was still a happy and healthy excursion, and at the end of the pickers' weeks of toiling in the countryside the colour had returned to the cheeks of all. From the tiniest baby to its old grandmother, they all had big smiles on their faces.

As the work came to an end, the pickers' hats would be decorated with flowers as they carried the last pole of hops in a procession to the farmhouse, a makeshift drum being beaten to lead the way. A feast would be held at the farmhouse and the farmer and his wife were toasted. Hop-picking holidays began to decline in the 1930s as more and more machinery was introduced and today there are no hops in Worcestershire. With cheaper imports, the fields were ploughed up.

The pea pickers in the Vale of Evesham were a mixture of local labour or visitors from Birmingham and the Black Country. The work day would start early in the morning, with the pickers filling around two or three pots each. They would then move on to another field, sometimes over 10 miles away, working all through the day.

There was a distinct difference between the locals and those from the northern area. The locals, who were employed mainly by the farms of the Evesham area, were dressed in blue or white with the women wearing big straw hats. The northerners, who worked over the parts of the Vale of Evesham where farmers wanted cheaper labour, were more uncouth. The women wore dirty shawls over their shoulders with bedraggled dresses and old boots. With their trousers pulled up to their knees, the men cursed the women for not picking the peas quickly enough. They had sacks, or soap boxes on wheels, in which they carried their belongings and they spent the nights either sleeping in barns or under hedges.

A Well-Known Motorbike

George Townsend started making bicycles in Hunt End near Redditch in the 1880s but in 1891 he ended up going bankrupt and two men were sent to run the company. Robert Walker Smith had trained in the engine sheds of Wolverhampton, while Albert Eadie was a salesman employed by a pen manufacturer. At first they received a contract to make small gun parts for the Royal Small Arms Company in Enfield, Middlesex. This helped put the company on solid ground and so the next bicycle they made was named the Enfield and they changed their name to the Enfield Cycle Company. With the arrival of the motor car they decided to have a go at those, and in 1902 they built their first one. Deciding to split the two types of vehicles, they bought new premises in Redditch to build the bikes and left the car manufacturing in Hunt End. However, their cars didn't prove successful and they closed the Hunt End branch. Motorbikes continued to be made in Redditch until the 1960s.

THREE WHEELS ON MY WAGON

Henry Frederick Stanley Morgan was born in 1881, the son of the vicar of Morton Jeffries in Herefordshire. He developed a great interest in engineering and studied at the Crystal Palace Engineering Company in south London. In 1901 he became an apprentice at the GWR railway works in Swindon. Then, in 1905, he opened a garage on Worcester Road, Malvern Link with a friend. Four years later he designed a three-wheel light frame and added a 7hp twin-cylinder engine. The Morgan car was born.

Morgan exhibited two vehicles at the Olympia Motor Show in 1910 but didn't receive many orders and his friend left the partnership. However, the managing director of a large London shop liked the design and decided to display one in the window. That shop was Harrods and together with a gold medal at the London to Exeter race, surely this would mark the Morgan for success. Sadly not. The problem was that the car was only a single-seater.

Thought went into redesigning it as a two-seater, and once this was achieved success soon followed and the Morgan Motor Company Ltd was founded in 1912. Production transferred to new premises on Pickersleigh Road and a four-seater family car was added to the catalogue.

EDWARDIAN MAIL ORDER

William Kay was born in Portsmouth in 1856 but came to Worcester to work as a jeweller and watchmaker's assistant. Eventually, in the 1890s he started up in his own premises and the catalogue company Kay's of Worcester was created. At first orders were made in person but in 1902 William began publishing a thick catalogue twice a year. In 1907 he moved to new premises at 23, The Tything. He died in 1927 and his sons took over.

With the outbreak of the Second World War the company looked for ways of helping the poorer classes afford the more expensive items. They hit on the idea of purchases being paid for on a weekly basis. The business took off and many years of popularity followed.

In 2003 Kay's merged with another catalogue company, Littlewoods, and in 2007 moved to Liverpool. The building in Worcester was then developed into luxury apartments.

The Suffragettes in Worcestershire

In 1908 the Worcester branch of the National Union of Women's Suffrage Societies was formed (NUWSS). Miss Power of Field Terrace, Bath Road, was the secretary. In 1908 a branch was set up in Kidderminster and in 1913 two other branches were formed in Malvern and Barnt Green.

On 31 March 1909 a group of thirty women tried to enter the House of Commons, saying they wanted to speak to Prime Minister Asquith. Nine of them were arrested and one of those was Florence Feek (1876–1940) of Pershore. Her father was the minister of the Baptist church there. Sentenced to one month imprisonment, she argued that she was a political prisoner, not a criminal.

Another Worcestershire suffragette was Elsie Howey from Malvern. In April 1909, dressed as Joan of Arc wearing armour and riding a white horse, she joined a procession through Hyde Park to the Aldwych Theatre. From then on she became a regular sight at various rallies. She even rode by Emily Pankhurst's coffin at her funeral.

Born in 1884, she had moved to Malvern with her mother in 1897 following the death of her father. In 1908 she began to promote the movement in Malvern and Worcester and joined a group travelling to London. Here she was arrested in June 1908 for demonstrating and obstructing the police and was given a three-month prison sentence. During her career she was jailed at least six times, sometimes going on hunger strike.

She eventually returned to Malvern but even though her health had suffered she did live until she was 78. She died on 13 March 1963 in the Court House Nursing Home, Malvern.

WAR BREAKS OUT

As the Great War, which of course became known as the First World War, took hold of the country in 1914, the workforce very quickly became depleted with so many recruits being taken into the army. It became such a worry to some employers that it even reached parliamentary levels. Leverton Harris, MP for East Worcestershire, advised Lord Kitchener that a request had been made for Horace Gee of Astwood Bank, who was in the army, to be allowed home as he was needed by his employers in the manufacture of needles. The request was not granted. No doubt there were many such requests. People had no idea as to the extent of the war or how long it was going to last.

At the end of July 1915 the commencement of the national register was announced. Everyone who was aged 16 to 65 was to supply their full name, address, age, marital status, occupation, dependants, nationality and place of work. If the form wasn't completed there would be a fine of £5, with an additional £1 a day until these details were handed in. On 5 October Lord Derby was appointed Director of Recruiting.

THE DAY THE WORCESTERSHIRE REGIMENT SAVED THE BRITISH EMPIRE

The Worcestershire Regiment dates back to 1694 and was formed to assist William III during the wars with France. A tradition tells that for a hundred years they wore their swords at mealtimes because, while based in America between 1746 and 1807, they were attacked by native Americans while having dinner.

During the First World War, 13,000 of the regiment's officers and men went to fight and only 4,000 returned home after many fierce battles. One of those battles was at Gheluvelt, near Ypres.

The British army was fighting hard to save a battle line that prevented the Germans from reaching the Channel ports. On 31 October 1914 the 2nd Battalion Worcestershire Regiment was resting at Polygon Wood when orders came through to say that the Germans had taken the line and were occupying the village of Gheluvelt. The order was to make a counter-attack.

Between the village and the 2nd battalion was a ridge, and the top of that ridge was covered with enemy guns. 'A' company stationed themselves on a railway embankment that gave a good view of the village. The rest of the battalion positioned themselves for a surprise attack, but it was a case of rushing through open fields at an enemy who would immediately start firing. 100 men or more fell that day but despite being outnumbered they got through and the Germans surrendered. The Commander-in-Chief, Sir John French, gave the Worcestershires a commendation in his despatches.

On 17 June 1922 a park was opened in the north of Worcester in commemoration and named Gheluvelt Park. Sir John French was asked to officially open it. Of the battle he said, 'On that day, the 2nd Worcesters saved the British Empire.'

Twenty years after the end of the First World War the Worcestershires were again fighting for the protection of their homeland. In the Second World War they once again suffered great losses in Dunkirk, Eritrea, Tobruk and Arnhem.

Some years later the British Army was reorganised and the Worcestershires merged with the Sherwood Foresters and became the 2nd Battalion Mercia Regiment.

INDUSTRY AND POLITICS

Stanley Baldwin, who became Prime Minister for the first time in May 1923, had been born in Bewdley in August 1867. He was a member of an illustrious family that had been established in Stourport for many years. In fact, if the Baldwin family had not made Stourport their home, it would probably be half the size it is.

Thomas Baldwin arrived in Stourport in 1791 to work at the Joshua Parker iron foundry. A hard worker, he was soon in a position to take over the works and began specialising in cast iron hinges. Soon known throughout the country, his foundry became the main source of employment for Stourport workers for the next five generations.

A dedicated Methodist, Thomas was unlike others of his time, recognising the divide between the employers and the workers. If there was a problem he didn't hesitate to go and help.

In 1825 a footbridge was cast at Baldwin's foundry that spanned the road between Tenbury and Worcester. It was considered to be Baldwin's finest work. Removed in 1966 as it was considered unfit for purpose, it was purchased by the then owner of Huddington Court as a garden feature across the moat.

When Thomas's sons took over they bought an established foundry in nearby Wilden and this was also to become a major ironworks. Then other family members established companies in Stourport. Enoch and Alfred Baldwin took over the factory once owned by Samuel Broom for the manufacture of carpets. Here they made enamel goods of all descriptions and used an artist called J. Darbyshire, who also worked for the Worcester China Works. His designs consisted of flowers, fruit and country scenes.

The family built houses, schools, a church and a hospital, and owned nearly every factory in Stourport. They were also responsible for building the village of Wilden.

Living in Wilden in the 1860s were two sisters, Alice and Louisa MacDonald. Alice went to a party at Lake Rudyard in Staffordshire. Here she met John Lockwood Kipling. They courted, eventually married and moved to India. When their son was born they decided to name him after the place they had met, Rudyard Kipling. Meanwhile, Louisa had stayed in Wilden. Here she met and married Alfred Baldwin, and their son was also to become very famous.

Stanley Baldwin was born in Bewdley but spent his childhood in Wilden. In 1902, he and his wife, Lucy, moved to Astley Hall. They had married ten years earlier. His first years in Parliament with the Conservative government were spent as Parliamentary Secretary, Financial Secretary and President of the Board of Trade. He was made Chancellor of the Exchequer but when Lloyd George died he took over as Prime Minister. He was re-elected in 1924–29 and again in 1935–37. He then left the House of Commons and retired as the 1st Earl Baldwin of Bewdley.

A GYPSY GODFATHER

Oliver Baldwin was the son of Stanley Baldwin and lived in Wilden. Born in 1899, he inherited the title of 2nd Earl Baldwin of Bewdley but did not follow in his father's politics. He joined the Labour party and served on the back benches for Dudley after the 1929 election.

Close to Wilden is Hartlebury Common, where a community of gypsies had camped for over a hundred years. One day Oliver was driving across the common in his car. He saw a gypsy running in the direction of Stourport, so he stopped to ask if there was a problem. The gypsy said that his wife had gone into labour and desperately needed a midwife, so Oliver drove off and fetched one. When the midwife arrived at the camp the man was so grateful he began digging under his caravan to retrieve some money. Oliver calmly said that he didn't want anything but if the wife had a boy they could name it after him.

Oliver often talked about the barefoot little gypsy boy who ran about the common answering to the name Oliver Baldwin Coleman, and how proud he was to be that child's godfather.

WORCESTER AND THE TIN CAN

After the First World War a new industry, which had taken America by storm, was to find a place in Worcestershire.

William Blizzard Williamson had left Wolverhampton in around 1855 and moved to Worcester. Here he founded the Metal Box Company using a few craftsmen he had brought with him. First he worked in a small shop in Lowesmoor, then in 1858 he built the Providence Works in Charles Street, specialising in japanned items. They were all decorated by hand and one vase could take four days to make. Women were employed to do the cleaning, varnishing and polishing, but complicated artwork was undertaken by skilled artists. By the 1860s the company was also producing biscuit tins and canisters.

When William died in 1878 his two sons took over and they were both to become mayors of Worcester, William in 1883 and George in 1894. After the First World War, George's son took over but the company was not proving as successful so he decided to try something new. The canning industry had become very popular in America and it proved the same in Worcester. In 1937 a new factory was opened in Perry Wood that eventually employed 10,000 workers and produced 2 million cans a day.

The birth of the freezer meant that canned fruit and vegetables weren't as popular, but people still bought canned drinks and pet food, so business wasn't greatly affected. In 1981 the Metal Box Company owned thirteen factories and employed 26,000 workers.

THE SECRETARY

Sir George Vernon inherited Hanbury Hall in 1920. Born in 1865, he was a character, a maverick, who continued in his unorthodox ways throughout his life.

His early years were spent travelling abroad. At the age of 20 he went to Mexico, returning for his coming-of-age celebrations, for which he was late. He then travelled to Argentina and then South Africa, arriving at the time of the Second Boer War. He joined a volunteer regiment and fought in the battles of Diamond Hill and Pretoria. He returned to Hanbury in 1905 and married Doris Allan of Shrawley. He was aged 40 and she was 22. They had no children.

In 1925 a 14-year-old girl called Ruth came to the hall as a parlour maid and it wasn't long before Doris discovered her husband dangling the young girl on his knee giving her elocution lessons. Doris left and went back to her parents.

Not long after that George went to Ruth's father and said, 'Ted I want to borrow your daughter for six months. Things are a mess at the hall.' Ruth Powick was now 16 and that six months became ten years. She learned shorthand and bookkeeping and travelled the world, being referred to as George's secretary.

At the end of the ten years George went back to Ruth's father and said, 'Ted, your daughter has been a treasure. I have decided to leave her everything. My one great wish is for Ruth to take the Vernon name. What do you say Ted?'

A change of name deed was listed in *The Times* on 17 February 1938 and Ruth continued living at Hanbury Hall.

On 14 June 1940 Ruth went to Droitwich. On leaving the hall she looked up and saw George leaning out of an upstairs window. When she returned one and a half hours later he was lying on a sofa with a revolver in his hand. He had shot himself. A note said, 'My heart is causing trouble at night, so instead of enduring what can only be two or three weeks more misery I take the short-cut.'

He was buried without pomp and ceremony, at his own request, in Shrawley Wood, which was a favourite spot as a child. Ruth was the only mourner. He had once said, 'No snivelling parson is going to read any service over me because I am not going to be buried in the churchyard.'

Ruth did inherit and on her death in 1980 she left £3,008,025. Quite something for a young parlour maid.

A SPRING THAT LIGHTS THE WAY

Herbert Terry founded his company in 1855 in Peakman Street, Redditch, in a small workshop where he made clips and metal fittings for use in crinolines. The company then went on to specialise in springs, to coincide with the growth of the motor industry in the area, and it was his son, Charles, who turned it into a successful business.

In 1932 George Carwardine inadvertently invented the Anglepoise lamp. Working on a new design for suspension, he discovered the spring not only looked attractive, but could be adjusted easily and was strong enough to hold a light fitting. He took the idea to the Terry's company and in 1934 a contract was signed that gave Herbert Terry the right to manufacture and market the lamp, leaving George to develop more designs.

Charles Terry was a teetotaller so it is rather ironic that the house he built, Southcrest, is now a large hotel.

INDUSTRIAL HIDEAWAYS

By the late 1930s war was once again threatening the country. With Worcestershire being tucked away in the central parts of England, well away from the threat of the enemy breaking through coastal defences, it was a natural decision by the powers that be to designate the county as a place to relocate, or build new engineering companies, under the Shadow Factory Policy. This plan was first suggested in 1935 but, as concerns grew that war was now imminent and therefore there was a need for more aircraft, the idea was developed. One of these factories was High Duty Alloys (HDA), which was producing castings for military aircraft in the south of England.

The parent company in Slough was already working at full capacity, so a 28-acre site was found in Redditch. Building on the new factory began in October 1938 and a huge Erie hammer, said to be the largest in Europe, was transported from America. Within ten months the factory was fully operational and it was officially opened on 16 August 1939. By 1940 2,000 people were employed manufacturing pistons, crank cases and airscrew blades, mainly for Rolls-Royce and Bristol engines. It was said that had it not been for the products of the HDA, the wartime expansion of the RAF might have been delayed for up to a year and therefore the outcome of the Battle of Britain may have been very different.

Other industries took on war work, with many Worcestershire firms becoming involved in the manufacture of armaments. Some in a most dramatic way, like the carpet makers of Kidderminster and Stourport. Even small garages took to making something for the war effort.

Worcestershire also became a place to store vital equipment securely. Fuel and oil was stored in the Timberdine and Diglis districts of Worcester, as well as Ripple, Stourport and Hinton on the Green. A disused railway tunnel through the Malvern Hills was used to store bombs, shells and mines.

In 1941, as a result of bombing raids on the Rover factories in the Birmingham area that produced aircraft engines, an enormous underground factory was built at Drakelow, near Kidderminster. When completed it covered nearly 300,000 square feet and contained 4 miles of tunnel. It mainly built spare parts for Bristol engines. Also near Kidderminster was the Summerfield factory, which produced ammunition. Two workers' hostels were built and the workforce came from all over, even as far away as South Wales.

WE ARE AT WAR ONCE AGAIN

Military control for Worcestershire came under the Central Midland Area Command. Its headquarters were located at Orchard Lea on the outskirts of Droitwich, a large house built in the early 1880s by the Rev. William Lea of Droitwich as his retirement home. Plans were immediately put in place as to what would happen if the enemy invaded, presuming this would be in the south-east. Using the code word Cromwell, Worcestershire was to immediately block all roads and railways. Trenches would be built in fields and electric fences installed, and any landing ground not needed by the RAF was to be destroyed or obstructed.

Norton Barracks, the home of the Worcestershire Regiment, was extended and large numbers of recruits and conscripts from both Worcestershire and south Staffordshire were taken there to be trained. It also became a depot for Midland Red buses, which were used to transport troops around the country.

In Barnards Green, near Malvern, the 36th Independent Infantry Brigade was given a home. And in nearby Blackmore Park, the 149th Field Regiment Royal Artillery was stationed. The 8th Battalion Essex Regiment had its headquarters at both Bentley Manor and The Sillins, near Redditch, and the 9th Battalion at Attwood Park, near Kidderminster. In summer 1940 the 11th Battalion of the Royal Warwickshire Regiment was stationed at Hewell Grange, Redditch.

So by 1940 Worcestershire was ready for the enemy.

Next came the airfields – Perdiswell, Pershore, Honeybourne and Defford. Perdiswell had been used for testing Fairey Battle light bombers prior to the war but, when the contract between Austin Aircraft Division and the Air Ministry ended in 1940, it was only used occasionally. To prevent the enemy from landing there, scrap cars and unwanted agricultural equipment were strewn about, which could be moved in no time if the airfield was needed.

Pershore airfield, which before the war had been a private flying club, was quickly requisitioned by the RAF and, using Vickers Wellingtons, Bomber Command trained aircrew here. They also used Honeybourne airfield after it was completed in November 1941. The airfield at Defford was completed in May 1942 and it was here that radar systems were tested.

IF THE WORST HAPPENS – WORCESTERSHIRE WILL BECOME THE CAPITAL OF ENGLAND

Should the unthinkable have happened and the enemy invaded and occupied the south-east, the government and the Royal Family were to be relocated to Worcestershire. Many large hotels and country houses were listed to be requisitioned where necessary. Madresfield Court was chosen for the Royal Family.

The Dutch Royal Family was to be given Croome Court, and Spetchley Court would become the home of Winston Churchill.

The Cabinet was to be split between Hindlip Hall and Bevere House in Claines. However, as this never happened, Worcestershire remained relatively quiet during the war. Certain parts did suffer from occasional bombing but nothing to compare with other parts of the Midlands.

OPERATION PIED PIPER

Overseen by the Ministry of Health, Operation Pied Piper was the code name for the evacuation of thousands of inner-city children, and in some cases their mothers too, to countryside locations away from the dangers of war.

In August 1939 the government designated Worcestershire as one of those evacuation areas and on 1 September the first evacuees began to arrive. Within two days 290 mothers had arrived with their infants. Later, 500 children were evacuated to Stourport. Other places also became homes for these children, such as Bransford, Malvern, Evesham, Clifton upon Teme, Broadway, Belbroughton and Bromsgrove.

As well as finding homes with local families, larger properties were also used. Rhydd Court near Upton upon Severn housed evacuees from London. For a short period Ombersley Court also homed evacuees from Birmingham but was later designated as a storage depot.

Madresfield Court.

Evesham, a quaint old town, offered a peaceful life for evacuees.
This is the old Abbot Reginald's Gate and Old Vicarage.

Coming from the urban inner cities, the majority of evacuees had never witnessed rural life before. Some had never even seen cows or sheep.

A PLACE OF SAFETY

Air raid shelters were built by the local authority, mainly in urban areas. Constructed of brick with flat concrete roofs, they appeared on many streets and open spaces and, depending on their size, could accommodate between twenty-five and 100 people. Factories involved in war work were all provided with shelters for the protection of their workers.

Many cellars under public buildings were converted into shelters. The ground floor of these buildings had to be reinforced by either thick wood or concrete to prevent those taking refuge underneath being crushed if the building above them was destroyed.

The Anderson shelter was supplied to people, on request, by the town council. They were free to those households earning less than £250 a year but households earning more were charged £8. Made of corrugated steel, they arrived in kit form and were placed in a prepared hole in the garden.

Some homes close to factories were given blast walls. Built of concrete blocks, they were strong enough to absorb the blast of a nearby explosion and protect the windows of a house.

THE REAL DAD'S ARMY

On 14 May 1940, following the 9 o'clock news, Secretary of State for War Anthony Eden appealed for volunteers to join a home defence force, to protect their home town should enemy paratroopers land. It would be an unpaid, part-time job but they would receive a uniform and armaments and they could continue with their present occupation and not need to live away from home. These volunteers were to hand in their details at their local police station. Within minutes of the broadcast men were volunteering all over the county. One had walked into Kidderminster Police Station before the broadcast had even finished.

Obviously the background of each volunteer had to be checked. No one wanted fifth columnists or enemy agents in the midst of the Home Guard, who were initially known as the Local Defence Volunteers (LDV). A large number of the older members of the LDV had been in the regular army so, during the early weeks and months, it fell to them to help instruct the younger members. Their main duties were to keep watch, patrolling the roads and lanes in pairs and, if landing by the enemy was discovered, to raise the alarm and defend their area to the best of their abilities until help arrived. River patrols were formed to keep an eye open at Worcester, Upton and Stourport.

Observation posts were set up and the best one in Worcestershire was said to be in the Abberley Clock Tower. From there you could see parts of six counties. Others were on the Worcestershire Beacon, Bredon Hill, and Ankerdine Hill. On a moonlit night the whole of the county could be observed. Where there were no hills, other clock towers were used such as Worcester Cathedral and Powick Church.

Many factories formed their own Home Guard, even the General Post Office, the Midland Red Bus Company and the Worcestershire Electricity Company.

Following the D-Day landings it was decided the Home Guard would, hopefully, be no longer needed so it was gradually disbanded. Worcestershire ceased operational duties on 11 September 1944 and the unused ammunition was quickly used up at shooting competitions. On 1 November the Home Guard was given instructions to stand down and final parades were arranged for Sunday, 3 December.

RATIONING

For most of the war and for several years after, ration books had to be used to purchase anything from food to clothes. The ration book held coupons for various items with the retailer's name, the one the owner was registered with, stamped on the book.

There were many reasons for rationing, but it was mainly to divide food equally so everyone was treated the same and had their fair share. It also prevented the waste of food and reduced its purchase abroad, therefore releasing ships for the transport of other imports.

9

A NEW MILLENNIUM
ON THE HORIZON

It took a few years for the country to get back to normal and rationing continued into the 1950s. Industries changed back to what they were doing before the war and returning soldiers looked for employment. Everyone got back to their normal lives as best they could. However, things began to change. The population was growing faster than it ever had, old buildings were showing wear and tear, and technology was making vast strides forward.

Some towns lost their link to the railway as Dr Beeching's report of 1963 led to the closure of many local lines. Some of these old lines can still be found in use as public footpaths or bicycle routes.

The church was no longer as it was. With decreasing numbers attending the services that hundreds of years ago were a way of life, many parishes began to share vicars and parishioners.

The grand houses of the seventeenth and eighteenth centuries were finding it difficult to survive. However, thanks to organisations such as the National Trust and English Heritage, many are kept alive for the public to see and we can walk through the rooms and up the staircases where some of our ancestors walked.

Museums opened dedicated to the industries and life of a past age, but even in modern times history could hold up progress. During the building of the M42 services at Hopwood in 1998, workmen heard a rumour that plague victims from the 1300s had been buried near the spot. Building work ceased while the ground was checked for any evidence of contagious diseases. Nothing was found and work continued.

OLD TOWNS, NEW TOWNS

With the 1960s it became the fashion to redevelop many towns by demolishing old buildings in order to build new ones and remove old streets to make way for new roads.

Ring roads were built to divert traffic away from the town centres and many town centres became pedestrian areas. New housing estates appeared around towns and in the countryside to house the growing population. Even shopping changed. Modern shopping centres appeared where the high streets once ran, and large supermarkets and retail outlets moved to retail parks built away from the town centre.

Although old factories were pulled down, many of the old industries of Worcestershire still remained. They moved to new industrial estates that were also being built away from the town centres.

The most ambitious plan in Worcestershire was for the redevelopment of Redditch and its status as a New Town. During a period of over twenty years, the facade of this small market town was totally changed. A large shopping centre, named the Kingfisher, is surrounded by a ring road and numerous other roads, dual carriageways and roundabouts, all leading out to the housing and industrial estates built in the adjoining countryside.

MODERN WORLD, LOST TRADITIONS

The year 1964 saw the end of a system of transport in Arley that had been in existence since around 1323, if not before. The Arley ferry was the last of its type operated by a chain or rope. The first documentation of it was in 1323, when it was then pulled across the river by a rope. Later a long cable connected to two uprights was used to secure the ferry, which had no power and was controlled by means of its rudder.

There was no timetable; the ferryman was on call between six in the morning until half past ten at night. The only people allowed to call for the ferry outside these hours were the police or doctors. People going to church, or children going to school, were allowed to travel for free.

There is no record of any passengers ever being drowned in the river on their journey, but three ferrymen are known to have drowned.

It was a very popular form of transport and very busy at times. One Easter Monday a record number of 4,500 passengers crossed the river during a sixteen-hour period. However, by 1964 it was operating at a loss, so a footbridge was built and the ferry disappeared.

SAVED FOR PROSPERITY

By the 1980s there were only three families still living in their ancestral homes in Worcestershire: Lady Beauchamp at Madresfield Court, Viscount Cobham at Hagley Hall and Lord Sandys at Ombersley Court.

The Foleys, Dudleys and Wards had gone from Witley Court, the Coventrys from Croome Court, Lord Hindlip from Hindlip Hall and the Packingtons from Westwood. The Plymouth family had sold Hewell Grange in the 1920s and the Vernons had given Hanbury Hall to the National Trust. Witley Court was taken on by English Heritage.

Of the ancient families of squires, only the Berkeleys of Spetchley and the Holland-Martins of Overbury remained in their historic houses. The Winningtons had left Stanford-on-Teme; the Russells, Strensham; the Berkeleys, Cotheridge; the Lechmeres, Severn End; and the Bearcrofts, Mere Hall.

One stately home rescued by the National Trust was Croome Court. The 10th Earl of Coventry was a lieutenant with the

7th Battalion Worcestershire Regiment and, as part of the Expeditionary Force, had been sent to France in September 1939. In May 1940 he was involved in the retreat to Dunkirk and was killed in action on 27 May at La Bassée. He was buried at Givenchy-lès-la-Bassée.

His 5-year-old son became the 11th earl, but with mounting costs after the war the family was forced to sell the estate. First it became a school, then between 1979 and 1984, the UK headquarters for the International Society for Krishna Consciousness. It was then empty for twelve years until an attempt was made to turn it into a hotel and golf course, which was not successful. In 1998 another attempt was made to turn it back into a family home. Again it was not a success and Croome Court suffered a few years of neglect. Eventually it was rescued by the Croome Heritage Trust, which, with the help of the National Trust, renovated it. The hall was opened to the public on 26 September 2009.

Ombersley cottages, which have lined the village street for many years.

Hindlip Hall also went through a number of hands until its future was secure. The last of the Habingtons to own the hall was William. He was a poet and when he died in 1654 he left no heirs.

The property passed through a number of hands during the ensuing years before being badly damaged by fire. It was rebuilt by Lord Southwell, who then sold it to Henry Allsop, head of the brewery firm Samuel Allsopp & Sons of Burton-upon-Trent. Henry represented East Worcestershire as an MP between 1874 and 1880 and became Baron Hindlip in 1880.

His three sons all had illustrious careers. His eldest, Samuel, became the second baron. Middle son George was MP for Worcester in 1885 until 1906 and Herbert, an officer in the 10th Royal Hussars, also played cricket for Worcestershire for a short time. The family moved to Wiltshire in the early 1900s and the house became a girls' school. Then, during the Second World War, it was taken over by the Ministry of Defence. It is now the headquarters of West Mercia Police.

Another property that was taken over by the police, in an indirect way, is Hewell Grange, the home of the Windsor family and Earls of Plymouth. When Ivor Windsor-Clive died in 1943 the family was forced to sell the grange due to death duties. It was taken on by the government and turned into a borstal, then a young offenders' institution. In 1991 it became a Category D open prison.

AMBRIDGE IN WORCESTERSHIRE

How many know the connection between Ambridge and Worcestershire?

In Inkberrow there is an old pub named the Old Bull and it was this establishment that script writer Godfrey Baseley used as a model for the pub in the radio series *The Archers*.

However, it is also famous through another writer. William Shakespeare is said to have stayed here on his way to collect his marriage licence.

The Old Bull in Inkberrow.

SPORT IN THE 1960S

Sport has been with us for many years, hundreds in fact, but it was in the 1960s that it became accessible to everyone as a spectator pastime thanks to television. For Worcestershire, sport has been mostly dominated by cricket and, in more recent times, rugby.

Founded by the Rev. Francis John Eld, headmaster of the Worcester Royal Grammar School, Worcester Rugby Club's first match was played against Worcester Artillery in 1871. The team wore white shirts with the city's coat of arms and blue knickerbockers.

By the 1920s rugby was so popular the club had to have an A team and a B team. After the war it adopted the name Worcester Warriors and went from strength to strength. They have moved grounds many times but in 1975 eventually settled at Sixways, near Warndon.

THE ROMANS RETURN

It was decided in the year 2000 that the area in Worcester known as the Butts would be redeveloped. The Worcestershire Historical and Environmental Archaeology Service began excavation of the site in August 2008 prior to redevelopment. Through these excavations it was discovered that Roman Worcester was much larger than previously thought and, in actual fact, was larger than the medieval town of Worcester. It was also discovered that the population was a mixture of Romans and Britons.

The evidence showed that the houses were scattered, with some having large enclosures for keeping livestock. Walls were painted and the floors were made of mosaic. And there was an amount of decorative stonework.

One of the first discoveries made during the excavation work was the amount of slag at the site. It will be remembered from earlier in this book that Andrew Yarranton applied for a permit to quarry the slag left behind by the Romans.

Another Roman relic was discovered in 2022 near Evesham and due to its perfect condition is said to be comparable with what has been found at Pompeii. While doing routine work, Severn Trent Water Company discovered a ford near Evesham. It is said to date back to the first century and marks on it suggest this 10m crossing was used by carts to navigate a brook.

THE LAST OF THE LORDS

One of the last of the great aristocratic Worcestershire families disappeared in 2017 together with its stately home. Ombersley Court, built between 1723 and 1730 for the 1st Lord Sandys, went up for sale after being in the family for 300 years. Lord Richard Sandys had died in 2013 and his wife in 2017. With no heirs, the property went on the market and was bought by a local businessman.

For one day, on 11 June 2022, the house was opened to the public for the first time in its history. Visitors could picnic in the grounds and view various rooms, which included the main hall, the master suite and the Duke of Wellington room, where the great duke had once stayed. The connection to the duke was through the 2nd Baron Sandys, who had been an aide-de-camp to Wellington during the Battle of Waterloo.

WALKING IN OUR ANCESTORS' FOOTPRINTS

For centuries our ancestors walked the paths and byways across the countryside to get from place to place. Now in the twenty-first century many of these footpaths still exist and groups of volunteers are opening them up, waymarking them and improving them. Kissing gates and stiles are being repaired or new ones erected to encourage us to follow in the steps of our ancestors. There are many natural footpaths left by our ancestors but two that go through Worcestershire are well-known.

The Millennium Way is a 100-mile trail that was developed by members of the Round Table to commemorate the new millennium. Starting in Pershore and ending in Northamptonshire, it traverses through places such as Inkberrow, Upton Snodsbury and White Ladies Aston.

However, the most famous of all is the Monarch's Way, which is based on the route taken by Charles II after the Battle of Worcester. It was a journey that took him six weeks, ending in Shoreham, West Sussex, and weaves across the country. It starts at Powick Bridge and follows the Worcester and Birmingham canal to Droitwich, before heading out to Chaddesley Corbett, Hagley and Stourbridge. Leaving the county for a short time near Wolverhampton, it then heads back to Dudley, Halesowen, Bromsgrove and Headless Cross, near Redditch, before entering Warwickshire.

Found on gates, stiles and fences, this circular sign
indicates the route of the Monarch's Way.

A New Era

On 8 September 2022 Queen Elizabeth II died at Balmoral and
the county joined the nation in mourning. Elizabeth had reigned
for seventy years and during that time had visited Worcestershire
on many occasions. Her first visit was as Princess Elizabeth
when she visited the Royal Worcester factory in 1951. As Queen
she came again in 1957 by sleeper train and was greeted by the
Mayor at Shrub Hill Station, Worcester, before going on tour
to Malvern, Kidderminster, Dudley and Oldbury. In 1968 she
attended the Three Counties Show at Malvern.

She returned to Malvern in 1976 for a change of name ceremony, when the Royal Radar Establishment became known as
the Royal Signals and Radar Establishment. In 1980 Worcester
Cathedral was the venue for the distributing of Maundy Money,

and then in 1983 her Royal Majesty was welcomed at Redditch, where she opened the new Millward Square in the Kingfisher Centre and the Forge Mill Needle Museum.

With the 800th anniversary of Worcester receiving its first Royal Charter, the Queen was once again a visitor to the city, followed in 2001 by a visit to the Royal Worcester factory on its 250th anniversary. Her last visit was in 2012, when she opened the new library known as The Hive.

So begins a new reign and no doubt Worcestershire will welcome King Charles III as it has done other kings and queens over many centuries.

BIBLIOGRAPHY

Amplett, J., *Collections for the History of Worcestershire. An Index to Dr Nash's* (1894, J. Parker, Worcestershire History Society)

Amphlett, W.R., *History of Worcester Glove Trade* (1925, W.R. Amphlett)

Atkin, M., *Worcestershire Under Arms* (1988, Pen & Sword Military)

Atkin, M., *The Civil War in Worcestershire* (1995, Alan Sutton Publishing Ltd)

Bradford, A. & Kettle, M.R., *Stourport on Severn* (2002, Hunt End Books)

Brooks, A. & Pevsner, N., *The Buildings of England, Worcestershire* (1968 edition, Yale University Press)

Brown, A.W., *Evesham Friends in the Olden Times* (1885, West, Newman & Co.)

Browne, E.O. & Burton, J.R., *Short Biographies of the Worthies of Worcestershire* (1916, Wilson & Phillips)

Cameron, J., *Worcestershire Through Time* (2013, Amberley Publishing)

Carpenter, J., *Victorian Worcester, a Biography* (2006, Brockhill Publishing)

Carruthers, B., *The English Civil Wars, 1642–1660* (2000, Cassell & Co.)

Foxall, A. & Saunders, R., *Redditch at War* (2004, Breedon Books Publishing)

Gaskell, E., *Worcestershire Leaders* (1908, Queenhithe Printing and Publishing)

Gilbert, N., *A History of Kidderminster* (2004, Phillimore & Co. Ltd)

Greaves, V., *Moods of Worcestershire and Elgar Country* (2005, Halsgrove)

Green, D., *Worcestershire & Warwickshire Life* (1974, Whitethorn Press Ltd)

Griffin, P., *A History of the Worcester Municipal Charities* (2020, Worcester Municipal Charities)

Gunn, S. & Monckton, L., *Arthur Tudor, Prince of Wales* (2009, The Boydell Press)

Gwilliam, B., *Worcestershire's Hidden Past* (1991, Halfshire Books)

Harris, A., *The Vernons of Hanbury* (2009, L. G. Harris & Co. Ltd)

Havins, P.N., *Worcestershire* (2012, Robert Hale Ltd)

Haworth, J. & Jackson-Stops, G., *Hanbury Hall* (1994, National Trust Enterprises Ltd)

Hemingway, V. & Haworth, J., *Coughton Court and the Throckmortons* (1993, Jarrod Publishing)

Hodges, J.R., *John Corbett – 1817–1901 The Worcestershire Salt King Volume One* (2010, John Richard Hodges)

Hodgetts, M., *Harvington Hall* (1998, Archdiocese of Birmingham
     Historical Commission)
Johnson, A. & Punter, S., *Aspects of Worcestershire* (1989, Logaston Press)
Leatherbarrow, J.S., *Worcestershire* (1974, B.T. Batsford Ltd)
Lemmon, D., *The History of Worcestershire County Cricket Club* (1989,
     Christopher Helm Publishers Ltd)
Lloyd, D., *A History of Worcestershire* (1993, Phillimore & Co. Ltd)
Macdonald, A., *Worcestershire in English History* (1943, Press Alliances Ltd)
Maine, B., *Elgar, His Life and Works* (1933, G. Bell & Sons, Ltd)
May, G., *A Descriptive History of the Town of Evesham* (1845, Whittaker
     & Co.)
Mee, A., *The King's England, Worcestershire* (1938, Hodder & Stoughton)
Moore, A., Curiosities of Worcestershire (1991, S.B. Publications)
Nash, T.R., *Collections for the History of Worcestershire, 2nd edition* (1799,
     John White)
Noake, J., *Guide to Worcestershire* (1868, Longman & Co)
Noake, J., *Notes & Queries for Worcestershire* (1856, Longman & Co.)
Noake, J., *The Rambler in Worcestershire* (1851, Longman & Co.)
Noake, J., *Worcestershire Nuggets* (1889, Deighton & Co.)
Poulton-Smith, A., *Worcestershire Place Names* (2003, Sutton Publishing)
Preston, N., *Wisden Cricketer's Almanack* (1963, Sporting Handbooks Ltd)
Robinson, J., *The Attwood Family with Historic Notes and Pedifress* (1903,
     Hills and Company)
Roelofsz, E., *A Millennium of History in Ombersley and Doverdale* (1999,
     Orphans Press)
Rollins, J., *Needlemaking* (1981, Shire Publications Ltd)
Schwarz, H & L., *The Halesowen Story* (1955, H Parkes Ltd)
Thompson, M,. *Woven in Kidderminster* (2002, David Voice Associates)
Tomkinson, D., Everett, D. & E., *Collections From the History of Worcestershire
     by T. Nash* (1984, Kenneth Tomkinson Ltd)
Tyndale, T. & Bradley, A.G., *Worcestershire* (1909, A. & C. Black)
Turberville, T.C., *Worcestershire in the Nineteenth Century* (1852, Longman,
     Brown, Green and Longman)
Wheeler, H.F.B., *The Book of Knowledge* (undated, 1930s?, The Waverley Book
     Co. Ltd.)
Whittaker, R., *Studies in Worcestershire Local History* (1988–1990,
     Robin Whittaker)
Willis-Bund, J.W. & Page, W., *Victorian History of the County of Worcester*
     (1906, James Street)
Wilks, M., *The Defence of Worcestershire in World War II and the Southern
     Approaches to Birmingham* (2007, Logaston Press)
Young, J., *The Centenary History of Kidderminster Harriers* (1986,
     John Young)

Other sources – the following websites were accessed between May and September 2022:

ancestry.co.uk

bbc.co.uk/WW2 People's War

britishnewspaperarchive.co.uk

englishmonarchs.co.uk

explorethepast.co.uk

findmypast.co.uk

history.org.uk

historyfiles.co.uk

researchworcestershire.wordpress.com (owned by David Nash)

revolutionaryplayers.org.uk

spartacus-educational.com

worcesterpeopleandplaces.org.uk

INDEX